RUN OR DIE

RUN OR DIE

✦

The systematic annihilation of the black man

Dr. Akeam A. Simmons

iUniverse, Inc.
New York Lincoln Shanghai

RUN OR DIE
The systematic annihilation of the black man

iUniverse books may be ordered through booksellers or by contacting:

iUniverse
2021 Pine Lake Road, Suite 100
Lincoln, NE 68512
www.iuniverse.com
1-800-Authors (1-800-288-4677)

ISBN-13: 978-0-595-37838-8 (pbk)
ISBN-13: 978-0-595-82213-3 (ebk)
ISBN-10: 0-595-37838-2 (pbk)
ISBN-10: 0-595-82213-4 (ebk)

Printed in the United States of America

Many of our forefathers chose to run in this foreign land rather than succumb to the debilitating grips of slavery. They would rather die running than to accept becoming a human commodity-for them, it was run as a man or die as a slave. And even when one or both of their legs were cut off to prevent them from running, their souls still ran and it is yet running in many of us today.

I am black, but comely, O you daughters of Jerusalem, as the tents of Kedar, as the curtains of Solomon.
Look not upon me, because I am black, because the sun has looked upon me; my mothers' children were angry with me; they made me the keepers of the vineyards; but my own vineyards have I not kept.

King Solomon
Song of Solomon 1:5-6

To Mama, who fought as a teenage mother to raise a man.
We grew up together.

And my girls: Nequisa, Keandra, Kayla

To those Negroes who purposely lost their identity in the transition
from Africa to American slave.

This book, in its simplest form, is a snap-shot of a part of American history, perhaps an ugly part, but never the less, definitely a part. History, as such, is often abrasive to some. It sometimes shows some unfavorable moments in persons or people. For that reason, it is oftentimes colored by the penmen whose attempting to unfold by-gone events. I am sure that is the reason why as a child I was only taught white American history in the public schools. I learned about George Washington, Thomas Edison, Benjamin Franklin, and a host of other white Americans. I only learned true American history (American history is incomplete without the black man) after I finished college-I had to find it myself.

We have to face our past or else we won't appreciate our present or be prepared for our future.

This book is not just about the past though. It is a call to a people to awaken themselves to a higher calling-to be committed to and responsible for each other.

It is not my intention to demean any man or group of people in this book; for I am one with all of God's creation. I cannot hurt you without hurting me. So, it is with love that I birth this expose' about us-black and white.

We have been duped to believe that we are better than each other, or that we don't need each other. That is a lie straight from hell. None of us are better simply because of the color of our skin, and none of us can survive alone—you need me, and I need you.

And, even though, I believe that he has been confused, and driven by money, sex, violence, material gain, and notoriety, I still love my white brother. Not a forced love, but a regenerated love. A love that says I forgive you for all of the mistreatment, and denial that you put in my life. This is the reason why Congress has failed in their attempt to resolve our deadly issues, Congress cannot legislate love. So, hence, I forge ahead to uncover and give light to some very sensitive issues that perhaps we are in denial about. In love I forge ahead.........

FOREWORD

As I take a panoramic look around me, I am engulfed with anxiety. Fear grips me and catapults to the deepest darkest depths of my soul. Like a jet soaring supersonically through an endless sky, dominating anything in its path, then suddenly, without warning, crashes untimely to the earth and bursts into oblivion as though it had never been. If we, as a black people don't change, as the jet, so will we-as though we had never been. Every race of people's life span has increased except that of the black male. If we continue at the rate we are on, we will be right along side the other animals who are in danger of extinction.

In 1960, there were 70 black males to every 100 black females. In 1991, there were 51 black males to every 100 black female. By the year 2020, there will be 30 black males to every 100 black females. And if we continue at the same rate, by the year 2080, there will be 10 black males to every 100 black females. And by the year 2110, if the Lord has not ended the world, there will be no black (dark skin) males.

Notice, I did not say that there would be no more Negro males, but rather, there would be no more "dark skinned" "black men". For as long as there is a white race, the African male will exist because just as there are no pure African slave's descendants now, the white race is mixed. 35% of the white race has some African blood in them. A blood line that started during slavery (the white master had sex with his black female slaves, and very secretively the mistress of the plantation would have sex with the slave males. Both would often time produced offspring). So the black male will be hidden within the blood of the white race. Because of that, genetics tells us that some where in the future, several generations, a white female will produce a black skinned male baby, or at least an olive skinned baby with curly locks of hair.

Because most things digress at a much faster rate than it progress, we can safely conclude that, with all things being equal, the dark skinned man will perhaps become extinct long before 2110, Whether before, during, or after 2110, the black race's genocide now seems to be inevitable unless alterations and alternatives are produced immediately.

What is causing this horrendous demise among black men? How can it be stopped, and how can it be not only stopped, but turned around are the questions that the black leaders and the black people must face right now.

Some readers may interpret this book wrongfully, therefore, I feel that it is of necessity to make some clarification before one commence to reading the body. First of all, this book contains a lot of history. And history, told as is, is often times abrasive, particularly to those who history depicts as something other than honorable. It is not my intentions to demean or subvert any race of people, for we're all brothers-I cannot hurt you without hurting me. But never-the-less, I've been careful not to dilute any portions of the facts, as I have perceived them to be, of history.

We are well aware that there is good in all of us. I have met a number of Caucasians that possessed good quality character traits. They judge a man by the content of his character rather that by the color of his skin. So when we say "the white man", we are not referring to them (although they are not entirely excluded).

When we say "the white man", we are referring to those Caucasians who pervert the law, maintain injustice and inequality, and who feel that because they are white, they are better. We are also referring to that class of Caucasians who call themselves Liberals. They turn and look the other way when they see injustice. I despise their hands off policy where they say quickly that they are not the ones doing the injustice. They support those that are suffering injustice only in thought.

This book was designed to awaken the black race and to give the white race a clear view of their sometimes mean and callous ways. We hope to uncover, if only slightly, the systematic plot to genocide an entire race of people. Whether intentionally or unintentionally, the program has been put in motion, and is operating right now-genocide the black male.

SLAVES WORKED FROM SUN UP UNTIL SUN DOWN WITH VERY FEW BREAKS IN BETWEEN—FROM CAN SEE TO CAN'T SEE. THEY BROKE THEIR BACKS TO MAKE OTHERS RICH

1

POST SLAVERY

It has been said that heredity plus environment equals behavior, or shall we say past plus present equal behavior. In other words, because there was a "then", there is a "now". One can not fully understand the "now" without measuring the "then". To understand why John Doe acts the way he does, why he is temperamental, moody, and violently aggressive sometimes for no apparent reason, one has to analyze John Doe's past, and there, you'll find the reasons for his moodiness, violence, and aggression. Sometimes John Doe may not even understand why he acts the way that he does. The "then" is oftentimes buried in the deep canals of his mind-but still very much present.

The fact of the matter is that the black people's behavioral problems started long, long ago-during their enslavement. What we see among blacks now is flares from a past calamity ridden people. Most of the black man's actions and motives can be traced back to his enslavement.

Why are black on black crimes raging? Why do babies have babies so often in the black community? It is because so often it's that person deep inside them who is still fighting slavery, still fighting for life, liberty and happiness. They are still fighting for self respect, still fighting for equality, fighting to show that he's just as much a man as any one else regardless of his skin color.

The person within must be brought to turns with the person without, Thereby channeling his behavior to a more positive manner. The person within is a black man torn from his native land, stripped of his freedom, dignity, culture, heritage and even his name. He has watched helplessly as his children were sold, his wife raped by his master, and he himself be used as a male stud-breeding other healthy black females (like animals). He was beaten senselessly on numerous occasions for trivial things. His blood boils with hate and the thought of running to freedom never escapes his mind. He is restless, angry, and agitated constantly.

The person without is a Negro (I suppose he's called Negro because he is not fully African. He has some white blood in his genes; therefore, his skin is not as dark as his native brothers. Negro is the name the white man gave to the Africans they brought to America. That's why Negro will always mean slave). He is a man that is faced with the ideology that he is inferior because of his skin color, and because of this, he is not considered a citizen or a second class citizen. He can't go back, nor wants to go because in the land of his fathers he is not accepted. His skin color is too light for them, and he is unhappy where he is because his skin color is too dark. He is in the middle-seemingly a man without a country. Pride, integrity, and self respect have been denied him. He's aggressive, sometimes violent, and indifferent and he will do most anything to change or forget the situation he is in. Whether by alcohol, crack, drugs, or whatever, anything to change or temporarily forget his state-even the slaying of his own brothers, he'll do anything.

To bring these two personalities together, the inward man and the outward man is the only means by which we can alleviate the black race's demise and bring them to a level of personal exaltation they have yet to experience here-to-fore.

◆   ◆   ◆

DECLARATION OF INDEPENDENCE

We hold these truths to be self evident, that all men are created equal, that they are endowed by their creator with certain inalienable rights. That among these are life, liberty, and the pursuit of happiness. That to secure these rights, governments are instituted among men, deriving their just powers from the consent of the governed. That whenever any form of government becomes destructive of these ends, it is the right of the people to alter or abolish it, and to institute new government, laying its foundation on such principles, and organizing its powers in such form, as to them shall seem most likely to effect their safety and happiness.

◆   ◆   ◆

THE CONSTITUTION

We the people of the United States in order to form a more perfect union, establish justice, insure domestic tranquility, provide for the common defense, promote the general welfare, and secure the blessings of liberty to ourselves and our posterity, do ordain and establish this constitution for the United States of America.

◆   ◆   ◆

The Negro was not included in either document. I only showed the beginning of each document to show its hypocrisy or exclusion of Negroes. They practiced slavery at its very conception.

From the crack user to the crack pusher, both are post slavery reactions. One is using cocaine to help him forget and the other is using cocaine to help him escape. The user feels that it makes him feel, just for the moment, that he is superior instead of inferior. For the moment, it doesn't bother him one bit about how people feel about him; he is in a world engulfed by felicity and he will do anything to stay there. But cocaine is a liar; it just distorts the user's perception while it eats up his brain! The pusher feels that it is a way to get out of or rise above this dismal condition given his race (so he chooses to become a part of the problem rather than the solution). Selling cocaine makes him lots of money and he thinks that money makes him somebody. It makes him just like the slave master because the dollar is the bottom line-or so he thinks. He feels that he can buy self respect, integrity, and equal rights. He too will do anything to keep this superficial means of escape. Both the user and the seller are deceived, for they fall into the same trap which they are trying so hard to escape. But, the seller is much more damaging to our community because he produces the supply that fulfills the demand. It is the crack and other drugs black dealers that enable the white man to stay in our neighborhoods without even setting a foot there physically. The black dealer is just an arm for the money hungry white beast machine.

Black on black crimes catapults from this "change and escape" syndrome. To change his environment or escape from it is one of the substances which fuel the genocide among blacks. Many men have been killed in black neighborhoods over turf. Why would John kill Joe because Joe is selling drugs in a place where John feels belongs to him—Is that not idiotic. Drug selling is wrong; it's a criminal offence. Now if both of them are wrong already, then why kill another brother over something that does not belong to either of you anyway. They will sometimes beat another brother for walking or entering their neighborhood. Why?......because they are caught up in the "change and escape" syndrome. In essence, what takes place is that, psychologically, the pusher who is in the "escape syndrome" would rather kill his brother and risk life in prison than to return to the psychological slave compound where he grew up. And the user would rather kill himself rather than to continue to live in the reality of "dressed up" slavery. In any sense, there is no excuse for its use. Drugs destroy what one is, and diminishes all hope of positive aspiration. As a people, we must say no to drugs. There is a better way. We must collect ourselves and become one. The problem has been that we have been fighting as individuals. And one will never beat this hundreds of years old system alone. We must stand together without drugs. Nat Turner, in his short fight against slavery, showed us that drugs and alcohol in a movement equals failure. Some of his followers got a hold of some apple whiskey and started drinking during their quest. In just a short period of time, most of them were drunk; the only one with a clear head was Nat turner-thus ended their revolt. Drugs and alcohol will destroy what hope one has. We will never win this fight alone. We need each other whether we acknowledge it or not. So, we need to stop tripping on ourselves and come together with one mind, one cause, one fight, and one win for the cause of humanity. We're all connected-white and black. The quicker we, as a nation, come to that realization, the better off we shall be; the harder it will be for us to be defeated.

It has been said that the black man ought to pull himself up by his own boot straps. He can't just pull himself up; for he has been swallowed up by gross injustice from birth. An injustice that is so large until it has permeated the land from the poor house to the white house. He can no more pull himself up than a man drowning in a sea of quick-sand can pull himself out. If the government had only kept their word (a mule and an acre of land) things would not have been as bad. How can the black people expect fairness from the masses of people when the government over-looks them? In 1865, our government passed a civil rights bill which was over-looked. In 1963, they passed a civil rights bill; it was over-looked. In 1965, they passed another civil rights bill; it too was over-looked, and during the nineties, President Bush vetoed the civil rights bill. It's no wonder that many Caucasians think that white is superior because blacks are simply over-looked at the Whitehouse, and that same mentality filters down to the local governments in every city. The federal government is often times telling us that they want the people to be totally governed by the local government. History plainly shows that local government has never worked in favor of black people, or shall we say more adequately that local government has never been fair, or impartial to the black citizens.

One of the first things the United States did towards their slave problems was Emancipation proclamation. It was merely a law that prohibited slavery in the southern states—the states that were fighting the Union. So, Emancipation proclamation in its truest sense was a slap in the face to all black people because it only addressed the black slaves in the southern states. Emancipation was simply a political weapon used to weaken the south and bring them to submission. This was, by for, a great strategy of war by Abraham Lincoln. Right now some blacks celebrate Emancipation Proclamation not fully understanding what really took place. It is such a wonder why so many blacks celebrate the day that whites gained their independence (4th of July) because at that time, blacks were still very much slaves. Officially, they said that we were freed in 1865, but actually, blacks were freed in the late sixties. I don't think that we can consider ourselves truly free when white men could beat, whip, and hang black men for anything from talking back to whistling at a white woman. When blacks had to sit at the back of public transportation and had to give up their seats, no matter how tired or old they were, to whites, could they say that they were free and believed it in their hearts. How could they say that they were truly free when they had separate bathrooms, schools, and water fountains in public places? No! Freedom was just a word written in congress to pacify the decent whites, black abolitionist, and ease their own conscious. How could they say that blacks were free when they were barred from certain colleges, bitten by police dogs for exercising their constitutional Rights? And even now, I wonder sometimes have things really changed that much? When a black motorist can be whipped senselessly with sticks and kicked repeatedly on national T.V. by men that represent the law, and the lawmen not fear repercussion. I realize that we've come a long way but we still have quite a ways to go.

When we look at the past and present, we see that black people are still fighting slavery. What has happened is that they took the chains off their feet and put them on their hearts and minds which is far worst.

Whether we as a nation accept it or not, the black race is suffering from a post slavery syndrome and some one has to be responsible. You can not take several generations of people and enslave them for over 200 years then suddenly free them and expect them to adapt to freedom and a hostile environment at the same time-no matter how long it has been. If you kept several generations in slavery for over 200 years, then it is reasonable to assume that it is going to take several generations and probably 200 years to liberate them from the effects of slavery completely-if, in fact, such can be obtained. I don't think that this will come, seeing that the slave's children, even though freed on paper, or still second class citizens.

If you take a wild animal and lock it up for several years and let its young be born in this domicile state, you will rob both the beast and its young of the ability to survive on its own in the wilds of the jungle. For instance, look at the pigeons. When they have been locked up for so long (they call it trained), even when they are released to fly where they choose, they will eventually fly back to their cages to be locked up and taken care of by their master who chooses which will live or die. So has it been with the black race; for we have been robbed unmercifully and our present behavior reflects the extent of this gross injustice.

Ever wonder why generally most black females are domineering, possessive, demanding, and overbearing when it comes to their men? It is instinctive, acquired from slavery. She becomes domineering because, during slavery, she had to be to survive. For her husband, the father of her children was often taken away from the family. He was either sold, beaten to death, or used for breeding purposes. She never new when her man would leave, how long he would be gone, or when he would get back. She had to become domineering to keep her family together as best she could. Overcoming her loneliness and physical needs, which when night fall came, her owner would often times come by and rape her, hoping to fulfill his and her needs, she took care of her family while having to work hard herself. So today she dominates, not understanding or knowing exactly why, but we know why-post slavery syndrome. Research shows that even during slavery, when the black female's man was home, she still dominated him; sometimes, she acted as though he wasn't even there.

There are a few black women who suffer traumatically from slavery today because they accept and believe the slave owner's passed down lies. Their enslaved ancestors were told that black men were but animals, unintelligent, barbarians with no aspirations to do anything, go anywhere, or better him self. For that reason, they court and marry white men. Remember again I stress that perhaps they don't fully understand why they have this innate desire for white men, but it's traced back to the "lie". One well known actress put it plainly on national T.V (Leanor Horn). She said that the reason why she dates and marries only white men is because she could not get the respect she wanted from other white folks with a black man that she could get with a white man. It is sad but that is how a few of our black females feel today. Now I am not saying that interracial marriages are wrong or mixed children are any less; one should marry who ever they fall in love with, and not merely because of the color of skin. What we are emphatically saying is that marriage only on the basis of white skin color is wrong and is no solution to this ailing problem.

Very traumatized white individual, whether physically or mentally, is suggested or given counseling and therapy to help them deal with their past trauma so that it will not interfere with the white individuals present or future. Why hasn't any one suggested counseling or therapy for the black people? Seeing that we never did get the mule and 40 acres of land the government promised, I guess we should not expect such trivial things such as counseling and therapy. I guess they (the government) feel that it's cheaper to imprison them, kill them, or let them kill off each other while they try to deal with their subconscious mind-a problem they neither know nor understand.

2

WHITEN HIM UP

All his life, he has been taught to be white, or shall we say taught to act as white men act. Many blacks don't understand what being black is aside from discrimination, injustice and neglect. The beauty of their smooth black skin, their dark drown eyes, and wool-like hair are black traits that the black race has been systematically taught to be ashamed of. Thus, some blacks, to whiten themselves up, they'll bleach their beautiful smooth black skin, wear contacts to change the color of their brown eyes and chemicalize their hair to rid themselves of that wool-like look. The end result is a black man with light skin, blue eyes, and straightened hair-whitened up.

It's quite hard to extinguish that "whiten-up" desire when it's buried deep within the individual's subconscious mind. In order to rid our brothers and sisters of this inmate desire to be "white-like" and to change the attitude of their neighbors about dark skin, we must first accept that we are black. Sounds absurd huh, but we can safely conclude that when an individual does things to change or alter his black characteristic traits which are common place to his race, then he has not fully accepted being black.

Forget about being "white-like". Blacks must realize that their black skin is beautiful, and because it is so beautiful, many Caucasians lay out in the sun all day trying to get a darker color. Until we, as a black people, realize that we are not inferior to any man because of the color of our skin, we will continue to suffer from the pains of injustice. We must say to ourselves, "I am black and beautiful. I am somebody. I am not inferior to any man because of the color of my skin."

It is no wonder that many blacks feel inferior, self conscious, and dissatisfied with who they are because our society collectively has put a negative connotation on that which is black. If it has black in its name, it is usually bad or worthless. For instance: the black plague, black fever, black balled, black out, blackmail, and black market. They even put on some of our foods—devils food cake is black and angel food cake is white. All of these things have a negative meaning towards black.

We must accept our person and fight to reach higher and press forward. Abandoning our slave names and acquiring African names and wearing long dread locks in your hair does not diminish any of the black problems what-so-ever. That is like putting new clothes on a dead man. The clothes will not alter his state at all. The most important thing is being renewed in our minds and understanding who we are, where we are, and where we are going, thus bettering things for ourselves, our children, and the black generation to come.

The degree of the color of a black man's skin does not determine how black or whiten-up he is for there are some blacks who have very dark skin but are ignorant to the black plight. And, there are other blacks whose skin is not dark and who has prevalent Caucasian features, but they are black to the core, physically, mentally, and psychologically—they are black and are aware of the black plight.

The reason why black women straighten their hair is because it gives their hair and look as that of a white woman. After pressing, her hair now looks like Mrs. Charlie's hair, so her subconscious mind tells her that she has to be better now because her hair does not look like the lesser people. Most of our black women will say emphatically that's not why they press their hair, and maybe they don't now, but its beginning started with, "the hair like the white folks". And, even now, we are prone to say that those blacks with curly hair have "good" hair. Why, because it's straight like the white man's is-and Mr. Charlie is good, therefore, any trait that we might possess of the white man has to be good.

3

RELIGIOUS SERVICE

As I travel back through the channels of my mind, I see blacks laboring in a hot field for little or no wages—Sometimes laboring for a place to live and food for their family. The papers say that they are free but in reality they are, very much so, still enslaved. He owned nothing, not even himself. He and everything he had belonged to someone else.

The White man could take everything from him and enslave most every part of him. He enslaved his soul, but he could not enslave or brake the black man's spirit-for that belonged exclusively to Jehovah. The soul of man is his intellect; his personality. The collection of intangible things which make him who he is, but that can be enslaved; thereby, altering or changing his personal makeup and making him become something or someone he is not.

No one can enslave a man's spirit, but a man can surrender his spirit (that unseen persona that connects him to who he really is). Thank God our forefathers did not surrender. Stripped of everything else, he only had Jehovah and Jehovah's spirit in him which was enough to break the bonds of physical slavery for ever!

Having lost all, degraded, rebuked, scorned, and chastened, the black race went to the hot fields, laboring from sun up until sun down with a strong belief that their deliverance would soon come. While they cropped tobacco, picked cotton, or worked sugar, they sang songs of praise. For many of them, singing was their way of revolting.

Their only hope, their only faith was in a supreme being—A divine personage that was an avenger of injustice. A strong belief and worship of the almighty God gained the black man's freedom, and it is only through strong belief and worship of the almighty God that the black race will remain free. If we allow ourselves to become defocused and dwell only on the material rather than the spiritual, or only on the physical rather than the psychological, we will easily slip back to where we once were because we're but a step from slavery now.

One of the ploys of the white supremest is to bring the black race to a state of mind to whereby he thinks that the more substance he has, the more he takes care of "number one", the better off he is. Such thinking on a broad basis will bring about his demise.

In our society, substance with no proper usage is called junk. So having substance (material things), and not properly using them will add to the black race's present dilemma. Yes, we need substance, for we can demand some changes because of substance. If we pool our resources, build our own banks, supermarkets, clothing stores, and be fair with our people, we can demand changes because of our pooled income and possessions-but substance alone is not enough. We need something that can weather any situation, and any circumstance-Something that can only come from within—for therein lies who we truly are.

There is a side of us that we often times totally neglect (the spirit man). The "spirit man" in us is our strength, but we have neglected him for so long until we forgot that he even exists. You see, man is a triune being, which simply means that there are three parts to man's make up; he has a body, a soul, and a spirit. All three were designed by god to work in unison with each other; one was suppose to feed the other; and so forth. The ones that are suppose to make us aware of our inner man and mature us in the ways of our "true" self (the church) has fallen prey to that materialistic monster. In our quest to build bigger buildings and have multi-locality churches, we're consumed by that which the eyes can see while our spirit man withers away day by day and moment by moment with each trial or storm that comes in our lives.

Our religious services have got to become a saving place of grace where we can pull off all our masks of pretending and hypocrisy, and allow ourselves to be real without fear of rejection or ridicule. We must keep at the fore front of our conscious mind the pressing thought "keep it real".

I am often overwhelmed when I think about how hard our forefathers fought to break that inferiority complex that pervaded the black community and yet we systematically make some of our people feel inferior in our materialist worship service. It's strange to see how black people fought so hard to be freed from the white supremest, and then turn out to be black superiorlist among themselves. But, I suppose after having been under the yoke of the white supremest for so long, it's only natural that he would acquire some of his captor's characteristics. Thus, making his fight to remain free and escalate his self-worth more disheartening.

The church must brighten their beacon lights that all that are oppressed, suppressed, and depressed might come, especially those of the black race. We must build the whole man-nurture his spirit, feed his body, and teach his soul.

Black preachers, for the most part, must let go of those emotionalized feel good sermons. We must address the people's problems, their pains, their wants, and their sufferings from a biblical perspective, in other words, the pastors must bring their sermons to where the people live their daily lives. It is good to tell me the story of Daniel and the three Hebrew boy; it is good to tell me about god delivering the children of Israel out of slavery; those are good stories, but we need sermons to come where we live in our daily lives, and show us how we can come up; thus, causing Bible principles to work for them. Just knowing that the Hebrew boys were in the fiery furnace does nothing for us if we cannot apply it to our own lives right now. It's not enough to know that "God can do". We need to know how to "get God to do".

But sadly, most black preachers don't have enough time to properly study; don't have time to properly address the every day problems his people face because he is forced to work a full time job plus. It's strange that the black people have immolated whites in many areas except in the area of pastoral care. 90% of white pastors don't work because their members demand to take care of his physical needs, so that he can properly take care of their spiritual needs. On the other hand, 90% of black pastors work because their members refuse to take care of his physical needs, thereby neglecting their own spiritual needs. They often times have this reigning mentality of "If I can work, he can work". So, they continue to walk in darkness because they have blinded the seer. Now, they walk in darkness and think that their darkness is light.

We must change. Our pastors must be full time pastors-no out side job. If he needs schooling, we must send him to school, for when we build him up, in essence, we build ourselves up. Too often, in the black church, the parishioners do not want the pastor to do well, and particularly not better than them. The mentality that pervades the majority is, "if I work then he ought to work", not realizing that pastoring is a full time job within its self. Notice what the apostle Paul says in the book of First Corinthians 9:9-14 in reference to pastoral care: For it is written in the Law of Moses,

THOU SHALT NOT MUZZLE THE MOUTH OF THE OX THAT TREADEDTH OUT THE CORN. Doth God take care for oxen? Or saith he it altogether for our sakes? For our sakes, no doubt, this is written: That he that ploweth should plow in hope; and that he that thresheth in hope should be partaker of his hope. If we have sown unto you spiritual things, is it a great thing if we shall reap your carnal things? If others be partakers of this power over you, are not we rather? Nevertheless we have not used this power; but suffer all things, lest we should hinder the gospel of Christ. Do ye not know that they which minister about holy things live of the things of the temple? And they which wait at the altar are partakers of with the altar? Even so hath the Lord ordained that they which preach the gospel should live of the gospel.

Paul was trying to show the church at Corinth the importance of taking care of their pastor's needs. This gives merit to the old adage that pastors use to utter, (As the church grows, remember me."

Churches fail to realize that God's anointing flows down from the head and then to the body. That's the reason why many of the black churches fail to grow. No matter what pastor they get, they remain just a small church with the same few members. Most of them want a preacher, not a pastor. So, religious politics and legalism has and is strangling the life out of many of the churches. It is quite hard to set someone free when one is bound themselves. We, as members, must allow our pastors to be the anointed, gifted men of God that we need them to be, thereby, we will meet our own and our brothers needs-white or black.

SEGREGATION

Segregation must leave the church. Congress has passed laws outlawing segregation, but yet our churches and pulpits across the nation are segregated. White churches are still white churches with a few token black members, and black churches are still black with a few token white members. If the church cannot impart with their color issue, we certainly cannot expect the world to settle the race color issue either.

I don't expect us to forget our differences for our differences are what make us who we are. Different can be a positive if we so desire. Our churches must reflect the new earth that John talked about in the book of Revelation. Note what John says that he saw in heaven:

Revelation 7:9: After this I beheld, and, lo, a great multitude, which no man could number, of all nations, and kindreds, and people, and tongues, stood before the throne, and before the Lamb, clothed with white robes, and palms in their hands.

John's statement seems to imply that heaven was definitely desegregated, interracial, and multicultured. We all suppose to serve one God.

I guess the problem is and always has been "what color is God". I suppose that is why we usually see Jesus portrayed in paintings as a very white Jesus. This helps to perpetuate the superiority/inferiority complex among even believers.

In order to be "real" about it, we must accept the "man" side of our savior as who he was-an Israelite, a Jew. He probably had olive skin and brown eyes because of the climate and genetics that we commonly see in Israelites now. Personally, I don't think God has a color. He's more of an entity than a person and more of a persona than a being. When we become consumed in the color issue, we lose sight of our true "self". How did complexion become such a perplexing issue among men and even in the church where complexion wasn't suppose to matter. The Bible says in Galatians 3:28:

There is neither Jew nor Greek, there is neither bond nor free, there is neither male nor female: for you are all one in Christ Jesus.

The Apostle Paul is emphasizing that there should be no differences noted in the church even though some of us may be Greek or Jew, or Hispanic or Asian, or Black or White, there should be no differences (even though we are visibly different) because we are all the same in Christ Jesus.

Scientifically, skin color came about by two reason-adaptation and genetics. God, in his supremacy, made man so well that man's body automatically adapts to his environment. For this reason, I personally believe that the first man, Adam, had dark skin, wooly hair, a wide nose, and brown eyes. Why, because if we read the book of Genesis, we find that God created man in Africa. I gather that Adam was created in Africa because of the mention of the four parts of the river that flowed inside of the Garden of Eden. Some theologians assert that man was created in Iran or Iraq, but I beg to differ. Genesis 2:10-14 says that a river went out of Eden to water the garden; and from there it was parted, and became into four heads-Pison, Gihon, Hiddikel, and

Euphrates. Note, Pison covers the whole land of Havilah (the Garden of Eden), Gihon compass the entire land of Ethiopia, Heddekel goes "towards" the east of Assyria, and the fourth river is simply the Euphrates. Now if the river compassed the entire land of Ethiopia, and only ran through those other lands, then it is safe to conclude that no doubt the river originated somewhere beyond Ethiopia-Africa. Thus, the first man was probably African (also the oldest bones that scientist have found of humans were those of a black woman in Africa).

But this, color should not matter. We're all one in Christ. There should be no differences among us because of color. So, until we, as a body of believers, can get our act together in reference to the color issue, we should not expect the "world" to embrace a love that can wipe away color differences.

Training Ground

The church also has to be a training ground for everyone. It has to be a place where young and old can come and acquire fulfilling knowledge. This is parallel to the old adage that I have heard-give a man a fish, and he'll eat for a day. Teach a man to fish and he will always be filled. So often times we take the easy way out. We'll give them money, or buy some food for them, but very rarely do we teach them how to live in a budget or how to handle their money so that they can change things for themselves rather than wait for a hand-out. Whatever professions we have in our church ought to be sought to train others in the church in some parts of this field.

As brothers and sisters, we're suppose to help each other along the way, so in turn, they can help someone else along the way, and in turn, they can help someone along the way etc.

Many of the poor cannot afford schooling. This is where the church must step in and help educate the under privileged. Many times we are expecting the federal government to do what our God told us to do-help the poor. This starts with us training those that are less fortunate among us. As a whole, we, as well as the world, ignore the poor, for the most part. Look at us, we have enough money to go to war, but not enough money to feed the poor; there seems to be something wrong with that picture.

We so often hear some of our leaders say, "keep hope alive", but I submit to you that hope without promise is not hope at all. It is despair. The church has got to become a safe haven for all of us-employed, unemployed, and destitute. The church must stop trying to acquire huge bank accounts and start spending the money as Jesus instructed-assisting each other and the poor. I am usually amazed at how many of the men in the church has changed the church from being an organism (gives and maintains life) to being an organization (a collective body of people governed by rules and regulations). I believe that is the reason why the federal government became stricter on the church; because it became just a business with huge bank accounts.

The church often times cannot become that training facility for the needy because sometimes they are fighting among themselves. You have quite a number of churches that have deacons in it that have no idea what is the job of a deacon. They seem to believe that their jobs as deacons are to protect or save the church from the pastor; so, thus, a fight spring forth between the two officers in the church-Pastor and deacon. The congregation is confused; they know who they should follow, but their allegiance and friendship gets in the way of their support of the pastor. So, you have some deacons, and of course other leaders in the church who feel like the only job that the pastor should have is that of just to preach on Sunday, and they feel that they should do everything else. So, hence, there is no time to "build" the church and put a training resource in it, because they are too busy trying to survive each other. Thus, they remain a church void of many Christian virtues, and rights, and abilities because they are too caught up in a power struggle, and the poor and any other needs of the church and its parish gets sucked up, or down, depending on your point of view, into this black hole of misdirected energy.

It takes all of us being on one accord to accomplish such a great task as Jesus left us-take the Gospel into the entire world, and as you go, feed, cloth, counsel, teach, preach, and love all mankind, particularly the poor.

It is virtually impossible to train while we fight each other. And they are not going to frequent the church when there is just as much hell in there is there is on the corner that the "thug" or who ever just left.

Our churches become hollow and tinsel without the plan of Christ. No matter how big and beautiful our buildings are.

4

CONFUSION

Sometimes blacks get so bombarded by their day to day toils until they become dis-focused from seeking true liberty. We get caught-up in materialism and trying to stay in the "now". It is kind of like what Booker T. Washington said when he first started visiting some of the share cropper's homes. He said that it was strange to see that many of the ex-slaves had pianos in their shacks that no one in the house could play, and yet they had no spoons or forks to dine with. They thought that having a piano made them "somebody" or made them more like "Mr. Charlie".

I often wonder are we still suffering from that I want to be more like "Mr. Charlie" syndrome. I see blacks driving expensive cars with nowhere to park them, or driving a Mercedes while living in the projects. I also wonder if the system has been design to keep blacks in that syndrome. Banks will lend blacks money to buy a 40,000.00 car, but will not lend them the same amount to buy a house. Even the church is caught-up in this loathsome syndrome. I've seen churches building a million dollar building while paying their pastor three hundred dollars a week which they know that he cannot live on-they expect him to work a full time job. There are even other churches that are in dilapidated buildings, the community around them is poverty stricken, and most of the folks are living in substandard housing, yet the church is spending thousands of dollars annually on a television program-he's on television grinning while his church is falling in and his community is dying. Usually this is transpiring simply because the church is engulfed in that "Mr. Charlie" syndrome. They think that "if I have a television broadcast, I must be "somebody"."

It seems that we are caught in a vacuum and can't get out. Blacks often celebrate holidays that have absolutely nothing to do with them—Holidays that usually demean us. A holiday is a day chosen to commemorate certain events or people. Why should blacks celebrate the fourth of July? That was when white America gained their independence from Britain. White folks became free from British law, free from British inhumane treatment, free from British absolute influence. The fourth of July 1776 was when they gained their freedom, so every year during the fourth of July, they celebrate to remember.

Now what are the black people remembering about July fourth 1776—That they were still slaves, still inhumanely treated by white America, still a commodity for whites, and still inferior to anybody that was white. The only thing blacks gained from that era is the introduction to the white colonist's religion (Christianity) which was not a true introduction at all. As a matter of fact, it was quite warped because they would pray in the morning and rape black women at night. They would pray at night and sale black men and members of their families at auctions in the morning; they would worship God Sunday, and go and burn blacks out of their houses on Monday. It's no wonder they established their "Jim Crow" churches-blacks sat in the back called colored section.

For too long, we have been fooled and lied to. Fooled to believe that we were a part of this nation (other than a slave), and lied to about this nation was built from a strong desire to serve God-at merely a glance, we can see that the early America was anything but Godly. This nation was founded because the colonists got sick of British unfair and unjust rules.

Some of the main reasons which prompted the colonists to seek independence from Britain were:

1. Taxation without representation.

2. In 1763, Britain passed a proclamation that prohibited American settlers from moving west of the Appalachian Mountains.

3. In 1764, Britain passed the Greenville Acts. The acts called for new duties and taxes from the colonists, forbid colonists from issuing paper money, and forced them to house British soldiers.

4. In 1766, Britain passed the stamp Act. After colonists resisted paying the taxes, it called for and threatened tax collectors with violence.

5. In 1767, Britain passed the Townshend Acts, imposing new duties on colonists for tea and other goods and giving British troops the right to search any colonist's property.

6. In 1770, the Boston Massacre took place. Bostonians, angry at British Acts, taunted British soldiers and were fired upon. Five colonists were killed (one of whom was a black man).

7. In 1774, Britain passed the Coercive Acts which closed the Boston harbor to shipping, and placed Massachusetts under military rule.

All of these were just a few of the reasons why the United States was born-not because they had this strong desire to serve God, but rather a strong desire to free themselves from the oppression of Britain-taxation without representation.

Now it is quite clear why our government allow laws against religion-Built upon God sounds better than we rebelled and started our own country.

In order the change our daily scenario, blacks must truly become a part of this country and realize that it was the sweat from our backs that helped laid the physical foundation for America. Pull off the confusion and walk in the light.

RESTITUTION

In 1865, all slaves were officially freed. The nation then realized that some sort of help or restitution had to be given to the former slaves. They decided that the exslave should be granted forty acres of land and a mule which would have been a great help because most of the exslaves worked well with the land. But this restitution never manifested. It was a promise, among many, that the U.S would fail to keep-forty acres of land and a mule!

Some have the audacity to say that blacks are sorry, slack, and slowful, waiting on a hand-out. They seem to think that the typical so called Negro is a welfare recipient or desires to be so. But they fail to realize that it is not that black people are sorry or waiting on a hand-out, but rather, a sense of owing is rooted deep within the subconscious mind of his very black soul. A sense that tells him that white America owes him something-forty acres of land and a mule. White America gave him land and a mule and before he could put his hands on it, they stole it from him. So, if anybody has the right to receive assistance from the government, the black people do. And although he has aspired much higher than waiting for federal aid, never-the-less, the government still owes the black man!

White America thinks that it is simply asinine and crazy to remotely think of paying the slave's descendents restitution, but it is quite understandable when we put all things in perspective. For instance, when the United States dropped a nuclear bomb on Japan, later, they sent millions of dollars to Japan to help rebuild what the United States had torn-up. When our nation went to war in the east, did they not send millions of dollars and man power to help rebuild what they had torn-up with their bombs, bullets, and missiles? Even while Russia's nuclear missiles were aimed at the U.S, we still sent millions of dollars to Russia to help maintain the Russian people (mine you; I think aid to others is wonderful, but charity begins at home). So, it should not be so hard for white America to understand their rightful duty towards the slave's children. If white America can help Japan, Iraq, Arabia, and

Russia (to name just a few), surely it can help establish the black race that has farmed their lands, raised their children, washed their dirty clothes, and cared for them when they were sick.

Before white America say that blacks are lazy and waiting on a handout, first give black America what you owe them; then they could truly help themselves.

They said, "Pull yourself up by your own boot straps!" How can we do that when often times they hold our boots and straps in their hands.

Now we see and fully understand why black youths find Malcom X statement "by any means necessary" so appealing. It seems that the only way that we're going to break this vacuum of hopelessness placed upon us is by other necessary means. The white man does not like black, nor red, or yellow, but he loves green. Green is a means that we, as black people have not fully utilized. They mistreat us; don't respect us, and yet we still spend our money in their stores; we still buy their products even after they publicly show their displeasure for us. We must change. We must show some control. We must demand our rights-boycotting is a very good way to peaceably fight.

Blacks are at the bottom of the totem pole of America not because they don't try or because they are lazy, but merely because they have been held under foot for generations after generations. When we look at some statistics this is apparent, the leading cause of death for black men between the ages of 15 and 24 is murder. If such a statistic was given for the white men of that same age, white America would have found the cause and the cure immediately. America is turning their head and looking the other way knowing full well the problem exist.

Not only are they looking the other way, but they are helping to perpetuate the problem. As I have alluded to on numerous occasions before, our prison system confirms this assertion. Blacks make up less than ten percent of the U.S population; we are a minority, but yet in the U.S prisons we are the majority. Simply by virtue of the population number, that ought not to be so. Because there are over ninety percent white in our nation, and less than ten percent black, it stands to reason that there would be many more whites in prison than blacks-there is a problem!

Restitution is far more than just material gain. It has to constitute much more—such as assisting blacks in changing the mentality that you (white America) gave us. I am sure that if white America gave blacks all their restitution in just money, in less than ten years white America would have it all back-the disparity would be back the same. Poverty starts in the mind. It's inside and pervades to the outside. I suppose that's why the business world calls us consumers, particularly blacks. Note what Webster's dictionary says of consume: To use up; to expend, to waist; squander; to destroy totally.

Yes, we are definitely consumers and we have learned it very well—particularly how to waste and squander. We must pull off being just consumers and begin building-up, saving, and restoring. It is a part of life to consume, but we must make it also a part of our lives to store, save and build-up. The reason why most whites have an advantage on blacks is because they usually start out with help. Their parents either transfer a business over to them, help them start a business, or just give them some kind of financial assistance. Black youths usually start with nothing but their clothes on their backs. We must establish ourselves to whereby we can also give our children a good start. Then, they won't have to expect welfare, food stamps, or any other governmental "projects".

A part of that restitution is helping us to help ourselves. I suppose that that was the intentions behind the affirmative action bill. It was design to try and make sure that the black race was not over-looked in jobs and in schools. But now, they are trying to get rid of affirmative action because white folks are beginning to complain about losing jobs or being over-looked in schools (I guess now they are getting a little taste of what many blacks feel like on a daily basis). If we get rid of affirmative action, we'll migrate back to the old Jim Crow standards of operation.

DESEGREGATION OR TOKENISM

So often blacks are faced with segregation in the midst of so-called desegregation, and the saddest thing about this is that the blacks are usually the only ones that's mix-up. That which we sometimes refer to as desegregation is simply racial tokenism. They give a few blacks a position and then declare that they are desegregated. That position is usually a token to pass the desegregation law and at the very same time keep segregation. When the company is inspected by the federal government, they can say, "See, we're not segregated; we made John a manager." The government passes it off knowing full well that John's position is merely a token. That is the reason why I cringe when I hear some of our statesmen say that we need to turn our affairs over to local government. Over-all, Local government does not work for the best interest of the minorities.

I am not saying that blacks should not strive to be successful or to ascertain that managerial position even though it might just be a token position. Change begins in singular numbers-one man or woman can start a change. I suppose that one of the larges problems in token hiring or positioning is that the black employee began to suppose themselves to be more than just that. So, instead of helping the situation of their fellow men, they began to become one with the "master". The successful black needs to put and keep everything about his position in prospective and try desperately to stay focus on the "big picture"-get the position but never forget the condition.

They say that we are integrated and desegregated, but are we really? No! We are still quite segregated. White schools are still white schools with a few token black students. Black schools are still black schools with a few white children whose parents can not afford to move. White neighborhoods are still white neighborhoods; for when blacks try to integrate a neighborhood, the white folks that can move out move-still very much segregated.

When blacks left the country and moved to the city, whites left the city and moved to the country and changed the name to "the suburbs".

The blacks that use to live in the "suburbs" can now no longer afford to. The reverse is slowly happening now in the city. White folks are now buying up the inner city and putting up skyscrapers and loft apartments. When the so called inner city blacks leave, they cannot afford to move back to the inner city because now it is too expensive.

They tell blacks, "Yes, you can live anywhere. It is your right." But, to stay within his desegregation laws, and at the same time have almost complete segregation, he moves to his suburbs and raise the price of land so high that only his white constituents and a few token blacks can live there. For this reason, many blacks, trying to grasp the total desegregation dream, focus only on their position rather than the collective condition. To be accepted among their white neighbors, they try to talk white, act white, look white, and think white. The only thing black about them is the pigment of their skin, and they are bleaching the hell out of it.

Whites, to try and keep their desegregation laws, and at the same time keep segregation, at their social clubs, where they have their social gatherings for white folks only, they say quickly that anybody can join; the annual membership fee is only $30,000.00—A fee to rid themselves of unwanted blacks. But still, there are some confused prominent blacks who will join these white clubs knowing full well that they are neither accepted nor welcomed. I think that if the Klu Klux Klans would accept them, a few of those confused blacks would even join them.

We have become too satisfied with being able to use the same toilet, the same water fountain, the same restaurants, and the same stores that white folks use. We must demand equality across the board and not rest until we get it everywhere, because injustice allowed anywhere is a threat to continued justice everywhere.

In one of Dr. Martin Luther King's speeches, he said that God had allowed him to go to the mountain top and see the promise land. Well, blacks have arrived in the promise land, but we fail to receive our fair share of milk and honey. As long as we accept or allow segregation in any form, we shall never dismiss governmental prejudice towards us-for white America's main concern is white America, no matter how you look at it. For example, they have taught us that the civil war was fought to free the slaves—wrong. The civil war was fought to preserve white America. The slaves benefited because they were one of the south's main commodities. It is like making war with Arabia; you go in and blow up their oil wells not because you hate oil wells, but because the Arabians economical strength is oil; so when one blows up their oil wells, one weakens Arabia. So it was with freeing the slaves in the South-it was more a strategy of war than a humane decision. We can only rid ourselves of discrimination by destroying segregation because where there is segregation, there will always be discrimination.

Thurgood Marshall and his associates fought long and hard to destroy segregation in our schools. He won the legal battle in 1954, but here many years later, segregation in our schools is still very much a fact of life. A 1993 study by the National School Boards Association reports that 66 percent of the United States black children attend schools with mostly minority students.

Some fools will utter that there is nothing wrong with being sepa-rated-education is education. If we lived in an equal society that would be so, but our society is far from equal or just. I agree with the Supreme Court's conclusion in 1954 that segregated schools are inherently unequal-their education is purposely inferior. In other words segrega-tion produces no class or second class education which is really a watered down educational system. Remember, we are still segregated; they just don't call it segregation. Our troubled struggling schools are in the inner city where the minority blacks are the majority-the whites have moved to the suburbs and started their own schools and school systems. Our government says that we can solve this problem by giving educational vouchers that will enable the child to attend any school of their choice. I don't believe in nor support the school voucher system. That's like putting a bandage on a gunshot wound and expecting it to heal by it self. In essence, what the voucher will do is leave the school alone and let it remain dilapidated and inferior. I think that it makes more sense to fix the school rather than give a few children a voucher. Make the schools better and you won't have to relocate and tokenize a few.

Because of segregation and unequal rights, black people are suffering immensely today. A third of America's black population lives below the official poverty line, as opposed to only 11 percent of whites. More than 60 percent of all black births are to single women, and unemployment has risen as high as 12 percent for black people.

When the inner city schools had mostly white children, the federal government support was 11.5 percent in 1980; when the whites moved out, federal support dropped to 3.8 percent in 1990-and I would imagine that it is decreasing even further now. I suppose that the federal government thinks that the only solution to the ailing black problem is parallel to that of the hypocrite Abraham Lincoln-deport all black people back to Africa. It is no wonder white America honors Lincoln's birthday.

What America must realize is that segregation disables and kills all of us. We can either live together or die apart.

THE NATURE OF MAN

As I travel these United States, I have often met some genuinely good hearted people. I have become acquainted with men that judge a man by the content of his character rather than the color of his skin. But even in them, I have notice a slight subconscious flare of the racial superiority complex. This is because we live in a white racist society with a very white system. So, try as they might, to rid themselves of the social injustice and racial mentality of their forefathers, they are still influenced and persuaded by the system their ancestors developed and maintained.

Because some white folks have been racist, segregationist, and discriminators for hundreds of years, it is now implanted in their subconscious minds. They are almost racist by nature. The nature of a man is the qualities or personality he seems to have been born with

The same subconscious nature is reverse in black people; blacks seem to have a subservient attitude towards white folks-they seem to feel inferior by nature, seem to look up and respect white folks simply because they are white. Many blacks feel that the degree of their success depends heavily upon their association with white folks. That is the reason why you hear some say arrogantly, "I live over there among the white folks," as if that alone measures their worth.

I believe that is also the reason why some of our black men date and marry white women-the white woman gives him better status; he feels that now he is somebody because he can say, "See, I got me a white woman." Subconsciously, he feels now he is just like Mr. Charlie. Mind you, I must add that I see nothing wrong with a black man or black woman marrying some one white or of some other different ethnic group; as long as they are together because of love and not just for color.

The white man is infuriated by the interracial union; he feels that the black man is not worthy of her, and that she is lessening their race-they hate her almost as much as they hate him.

Neither race is born with the superior, inferior personality. It is taught to them; whether consciously or subconsciously, it is, never-the-less, taught. The child will always immolate those around him. It is like the welfare syndrome. Statistics show that sometimes welfare recipients will have three and four generations receiving welfare (mind you, there are for more whites on welfare than there are blacks). Somewhere, the succeeding welfare recipient's generation was taught, whether directly or indirectly, that welfare was the only means of life support and maintenance. Therefore, each generation reached no higher, or expected no more than welfare. Their thought is, "One day I will be able to get a welfare check like Mama."

If from a child a man has been taught that he is superior because of his race, then he will feel that way until he is taught otherwise or until he comes face to face with reality. And even in the midst of teaching and reality, he will still harbor that superiority complex deep within his subconscious mind.

It is the complete reverse with blacks. Reality shows him that he is not any less simply because of the color of his skin, for he can run just as fast or faster; he can jump just as high or higher, and he can think just as well or better. Reality shows him that it is his soul and mind that make him different from others-not the color of his skin. But sadly, even amidst reality many blacks still subconsciously harbor that inferiority complex-with a lot of help from the white system. Both races suffer because of their learned complex personalities. The only way either will deviate from their nature is through continuous counseling. And although white folks can be counseled, their reframing from their dogmatic superiority complex is almost an impossibility.

One can always convince a humble people to come up, but it is quite a task to convince an exalted people to come down. Power is never just readily given up. It is always taken. No ruler or people will ever abdicate their position of authority on their own-no matter how obnoxious or wrong they are.

Even if white America fails to change (which is almost certain), blacks must strive for change and exaltation—We cannot settle for less. Blacks are only a step from slavery right now because when a man can manipulate ones mind, the body is certain to follow.

Because subconsciously many black people are suffering from the inferiority complex, we must promote and educate our people to a higher level of self worth. We must not allow ourselves to be pushed back any further. Because injustice and mistreatment pervades and permeates our ranks at an escalating rate, we must stand firm in our belief that God is on our side and is with us during these trying times. "Right" will prevail. Good has always overcome evil, but not by passive means. We must be aggressive. We must channel and focus our aggression to our own exaltation and liberation. It is time to stop singing, "We shall over come"; it is time for us to come over. We must look beyond the sound good speeches like "keep hope alive" for they tell us to wait and hope that things will get better (remember, hope without promise is not hope at all; it is despair). Time has taught us that white folks "wait" means "never". Blacks must adamantly desire to eat of all the milk and honey of this promise land which our forefathers help to build. And for us to sit around and wait for other folks to change things for us, is like a lamb waiting for a wolf to teach it how to avoid being eating by a wolf-that would be a pretty stupid lamb wouldn't you say.

As long as we live in a capitalistic society, there will always be "slaves" and "masters". Capitalism produces segregation in and of it self because there will be people having more than others; therefore, the separation is automatically systematic—The have not, the have, and the have more. Thus, we are divided by affluent neighborhoods, and distinguished by the kinds of cars we drive, and the kinds of clothes we wear. This is the trend among the whites; it's even worse among the blacks because whatever happens in their lives rolls down this capitalistic segregated latter to black folks. When it gets to blacks, it is always magnified. It's the snow ball effect; it starts with the "have more" as a pebble, but by the time it reaches the blacks, it's a boulder.

Blacks suffer more because of this capitalistic segregation. That's why we find many who drive expensive cars while living in shacks; their car costs more than their house—If they have a house at all. Is it conceivable to drive a new car while living in the "projects"?

Why will we pay $150.00 for a pair of sneakers and struggle to buy our babies diapers and milk; why, because blacks are caught-up in the capitalistic segregational system. They feel like the more "stuff" they have, the more self worth they'll have. Little do they realize, this thinking perpetuates the "slave" "master" syndrome because the white man realizes the black's thinking so he produces more pretty "stuff" for him to buy, thereby producing a paradox—much stuff, but still poor. Kind of like what the white man did to the Indians that owned parts of New York; they bought it from the Indians with some pretty beads and a few fur skins.

This is the reason why it is easier for blacks to get a loan for an expensive new car than for a new house. The white system gives him what it takes to help him remain in the system. If he buys the house, it builds up equity and increases in value; the new car, no matter what kind it is, as soon as it leaves the lot, it decreases in value and soon, very soon, he'll have to go buy another one to remain in the "new".

Because of this capitalistic produced segregation, black young adults usually start behind with little or no help as opposed to their white counter parts. This capitalistic mind will always allow us to allow someone else to choose our destiny for us.

We're so busy giving our money back to the white man until we haven't paused long enough to develop our own collective economical strength. Capitalism is so enveloping until it even caused us to form segregation among ourselves. Capitalism dictates fiscal responsibility be somebody else's problem and money be spent as quickly as it is earned on material things that can produce status among peers. That's why the blacks spend their money on nonessential high priced commodity goods such as Air Jordan's, Nikes, Adidas, Polo, Tommy Hilfiger, Guess, Timberland, Shawn John, and an endless host of other manufacturers. To acquire this "status" commodity, many engage in illegitimate enterprise to enable themselves to become "somebody".

Segregation is such the norm in America; Booker T. Washington tried to rationalize it. He said that we can be as together as the hand, but as separate as the fingers. I believe that Washington felt this way for two reasons: 1) He was trying to please his white constituents. 2) He was trying to persuade blacks to accept things the way they were and not try to change things.

I strongly disagree with Mr. Washington's views. Segregation always produces discrimination; one never exists without the other. We must not accept and we must not compromise. Blacks tried running from the issue before in the past. They seemed to think that segregation and racism were southern problems so they migrated north only to be confronted with the same problem; during the 1950s, 100,000 black folks migrated to Baltimore, and during that same period, 183,000 migrated to Detroit. They found that America was white every where-created by the white man for the white man. If you were from any other ethnic group (non white), you were a second class citizen.

True change must start inside and manifest outside until the whole has changed. The most wonderful thing about change is that it is contagious-if one changes, another one will, and other one will etc.

The white system of capitalism is so harsh until it even sucks in many of their own kind. The white capitalistic system was not designed to assist, maintain, or make life better for blacks or average to poor whites. They designed a system that enabled their citizens to spend tomorrow's money today and charge them compound interest on it-they call it credit. Most of us do not even stop to think on our own; we just take what Mr. Charlie tells us at face value. Most of us really believe that we are paying 5-8% interest on our mortgages. The only way that you pay 5-8% interest is that you pay the house off the first month you acquire it. Most 30 year mortgages, if you make the scheduled payments, charge you 300% interest. It's like this, when you have paid your last payment, you will have paid your lender three times what he loaned you-a $100,000.00 house will actually cost you a little over $3oo,000.00 (300%)-you do the math. If one was truly paying 5-8% on their loan then the least they would repay is $105,000.00, and the most would be $108,000.00. The capitalistic system was designed to keep you enslaved (economically); it takes money to be free. I must admit, though, that the white man is very clever. He tells you that it is very important that you keep good credit so he rates you on a credit scale. He tells you to keep a good credit score and you can get whatever you want. Thus, it is an unending debt story because you are always trying to keep a good score. You'll never let one bill go late while you payoff another because it will damage your score-so you continue to pay "on" all your bills on time so as to keep a good score-which is designed to keep you in debt for 20-30 years. On a $5000.00 credit card, if you pay them back on time and keep your score good, you will owe them for about 40 years and end up paying them about 40-$60.000.00.

The white system is a machine made to roll over you and keep you bound and indebted in "the system". The ultimate paradox is we are free slaves. We are an up-scale share cropper with prettier things. And, just like the original share cropper, the system is designed to keep us in the system. The original share cropper stayed on Mr. Charlie's land, and when he was paid, he shopped at Mr. Charlie's store (his bill was usually put on a tab which he never could break even or pay off). We're in the same system; the names are changed, but none the less, it's the same. You'll never get out accidentally.

5

Hate Begets Hate

Earnest Hemingway once quoted a most thought provoking phrase. He said, "No man is an island apart to himself. Every man is a part of the main. If my brother dies, it diminishes me." That was quoted in part. Hemingway was saying that whether we like it or not, all of us are a part of each other (white or black). We need each other. We will either live together or die apart.

If a man hates any man for any reason, he will soon bring about his own destruction; for hate destroys the one whose bosom it nestles. Black people should not bring themselves to hate any man. Even though our blood has been shed senselessly from one part of this country to another, we must not hate; even though they have hanged our fathers, raped our mothers and grandmothers, and took our grandfather's manhood so completely until, here, generations later, we are still suffering from what they did to great granddaddy. We still must not hate. Even though they have assassinated or destroyed our black leaders who were the pillars of our freedom-Marcus Garvey, Malcom X, Martin Luther King, etc—we must not hate, and even though, right now, we are treated as second class people, beaten, scorned, imprisoned, and denied equal rights, we must not hate!

Hate will take us farther from equal rights. Hate will take us back to Memphis Tennessee in 1968 where Martin Luther King Jr. felt the sting of an assassin's bullet, back to Harlem New York in February 1965 where Malcom X's last drops of blood was spilled by his own brothers and conspirators, back to Africa in 1619 where our forefathers were herded up like animals by each other to sale to the white slave trader. No, we must not allow ourselves to regress; we must progress to highs that we have only dreamed about here-to-fore.

Hate produces hate, and the end result of hate is destruction, failure and degradation. We must think longer; see farther, so that our dreams might become a reality. The hater can see no further than what he can physically see, can dream only of yesterday and his realities are fogged by his emotions.

Now is the time for black people every where to rise to the occasion. The bells of freedom are ringing louder than they were in 1865 when blacks were declared free, louder than they were in 1954 when the Supreme Court declared it unlawful to have segregated schools, and still even louder than they were in 1965 when the civil rights bill was passed. Our souls are burning from the echoes of freedom bells.

There is a stirring among black people. It is as though a giant is about to awaken from a deep terrible sleep. We have become tired of waiting. The ironic thing about it all is that white racists want to keep the black giant asleep, but their hate and jealousy won't allow them. They keep kicking him, beating him, and every kick stirs the black giant even more.

Blacks have learned two very important things from white folks if we have not learned anything else: hate will destroy a man and jealousy will enrage a man. So when we stand unwavering for our complete rights, we shall stand without the chains of hate.

White America has distaste for blacks because of who they are and what they represent. The great misconception is that blacks are hated only because of the color of their skin. Such a statement is not entirely true. While skin color plays a part, there are deeper issues that fuel the racist machine. If it was just because of skin color, those blacks whose skin was almost white or high yellow would have no problem-but of course they do. As soon as white folks realize that that light complexion has what they call "Negro blood" in them, immediately, or soon after, they experience prejudice, discrimination and segregation; so it is not a matter of having darker skin. It is a matter of being a Negro. There are many nationalities with dark skin that white America doesn't systematically hate. The reason why dark skin is so profoundly discriminated against by white folks in the United States is because to them that black skin is a strong indication that that person is in fact a Negro. Hence, the fact of the matter is not being black; it is being a Negro.

The reason why white folks are so irritated at the sight or thought of the "negro" is because Negroes are an unpleasant reminder to them. As long as the black man remain, they can't claim to be all decent, good, an up-right. Black folks remind the white man of how low-down he has been (I believe that is why Abraham wanted congress to give them a free trip back to Africa). The mere appearance of a Negro dissolves the white man's allusion of his nobility and respectability. When the white man sees a Negro, he also sees a race of people that he has misused, abused and exploited for his own gain and pleasure.

Men do well as long as their skeletons remain in the closet. But because of his God given conscious, man fines strong discomfort when his skeletons are facing him daily. In essence, all the white man wants to do is get rid of the reminders or completely justify their inhumane actions. That is the reason why they often say, "Go back to Africa"-to get rid of their skeletons. For the above cause, they tried adamantly to convince the exslaves to board a ship free of charge and go back to Africa. America financed this voyage. They sent them to a place that the slaves started calling Liberia (meaning place of freedom).

White American supremest hate blacks because of who they are and by the same margin, they are fearful of blacks because of what they are. Blacks adaptability is incredible. We have been to hell and back and are still able to press our way onward, still able to stand along side those that sent us to hell unmoved. We have stood the test, weathered the storm, and still have risen above the racist beast.

As I take a panoramic view of the situation as a whole, I can fully understand why white folks hate blacks so much. I can fully understand why they are jealous of blacks. For you see, if I had misused, abused, exploited, manipulated, and killed a race of people of whom I presently lived among, if I saw that their adaptability was remarkable, their strength incredible, their courage immeasurable, and if I saw them getting stronger day by day, then I too would perhaps hate them and try to get rid of them. Because deep in the crevasses of my mind would lie the thought of the conqueror being conquered, or he who use to be master will soon be slave; I guess that I would do all that I could do to stop the inescapable.

The white man's fear and hate is unfounded. We don't want to conquer any man, for we know what it feels like to be conquered. We don't want to enslave any man, for we know what it feels like to be a slave. We just want to be treated fairly, equally and humanly. We want it to be where we and our children can exercise every right we have as United States citizens just like everybody else.

NIGGER/NEGRO

When we look at the race of black people, we see more than just "black" people. We notice that the black race is very colorful-from dark black to high yellow and everything in between. This is because he has a mixture of white blood in him. During slavery, the slave owner and his wife often used the slaves to relieve their own sexual desires; thus came forth what was commonly called mulattoes-half black and half white. While it was not very common for the master's wife to have relations with the slave man, however it did sometimes occur. These babies that the slave owner's wife had from the slave were often killed at birth, but on the other hand, the babies that the slave woman had from the owner were often allowed to live and grow up as a slave with privileges-but still a slave.

Color difference is one of the many reason for separation among black people. We discriminate against each other because of something we as individuals had no control over-skin color. But, non-the-less, we are divided because of this skin variation. White America, seeing that division, classified us-Nigger and Negro.

To white America, Nigger (which is the twin of Negro) was the lowest thing on the face of the earth. To them, it was not a he or she; Nigger was an "it". Something to be used, sold or bought like any other commodity. A Nigger is void of respect, inhuman, uncivilized, and unintelligent. He does not deserve any rights, civil or otherwise. He is an animal that should be treated as such. Nothing is lower than a Nigger; that's what white America means when they use that one word-Nigger.

Make no mistake, when they say Nigger, they are speaking only of some black person. I have heard some of my people use the word Nigger casually and try to justify their usage by saying, "It's nothing; anybody can be a Nigger." Such a fool deceives himself. For when white America uses the word Nigger or hears the word Nigger, they are referring to or reminded of a black person. When we use the word Nigger, that is, in fact, who we are referring to also.

We should never stoop so low as to refer to one another as Nigger; for we are not now Niggers nor ever have been or ever will be. At one time it was hip to address one another by saying, "What's up my Nigger?" or "My Nig." Such foolishness must always be swiftly put away from among us. Black people should not use Nigger among themselves, and they should not allow their white friends or associates to use the word Nigger-not ever; for others will only respect you to the degree that you respect yourself.

While Nigger had a denouncing connotation (and still does), Negro, on the other hand, has a more bearing connotation. To white folks in North America, Negro meant a slave who has been freed and has adjusted quite well to his white superiors. Not only has the Negro adapted, but even more sickening is that he has accepted discrimination, segregation, and inhuman treatment (that's what Booker T. Washington was teaching-be happy being a Negro). He has denounced his black heritage. He degrades himself and spends all of his time trying to be white and chasing after the American dream-become a capitalistic aristocrat.

You see, the reason why white America gave blacks the name Negro was to continue to cut off or kill his heritage (remember, one of the first things that the owner did to the slave when he arrived was give him an American name. He would be beaten if he referred to himself or his associates by their African name). Negro, as is, only roots are that of a former slave, and even now, second class citizenship.

White supremest do not want the black man to trace himself back to the Ethiopian Empire or his Egyptian heritage because if he does, he will know that he has for more to be proud of; he can truly be black and proud.

The white man took four essential things from the black man upon capture and enslavement; he took his name, physical freedom, heritage, and culture. Since emancipation, the only thing that he has gotten back is some of his physical freedom.

They call him the American Negro-he is an American; a United States citizen. But is he really? Because he is an American, we don't have to pass any laws to make sure the white man lives where he wants to. Because he is an American, we don't have to pass any laws to enable the white man to vote. Because he is an American, we don't have to pass any laws against discrimination, segregation, and civil rights for the white man—because he is an American. The so called American Negro of today was born in America. His father and grandfather was born in America, and according to the laws, if one was born in America, they are automatically an American citizen. Thus, the black man is an American citizen with all the rights that citizenship affords. So why do America has to pass laws to give the black man rights that he suppose to already have if he is already an American citizen; the reason, his citizenship was never recognized. It was more or less forfeited because of who he was and the color of his skin.

The 13th amendment freed him; the 14th made him a citizen, and the 15th gave him the right to vote. But, they still have to pass laws and fight so that the American Negro citizen can live where he wants to, vote how he wants to without discrimination and malice. If the Negro was truly a citizen, he would automatically have certain inalienable rights (sounds familiar, that is what they declared to Britain in the constitution). What they really meant was that all white men had certain inalienable rights.

Although he was born here, raised here, and helped build this country by the sweat of his brow, the black man is still not an equal citizen with equal rights or how else can one explain the violent beating of blacks on national T.V by policemen. The policemen do it because they fear little or no consequences by the public or the judicial system.

WHITE JUSTICE

The Black race can stop waiting for equal justice from the present judicial system. It will never come. The only kind of justice that black people will get in this country is white justice, and white justice for black men is not justice at all. The judicial system which we are presently governed by was designed and instituted by the white man for the white man.

In the Declaration of Independence, they say something to the effect that all men are created equal and are due certain inalienable rights from their creator, among them are life, liberty, and the pursuit of happiness. Were blacks included?

The constitution says that American citizens have freedom of speech and freedom of religion. They meant only for white America; for if they truly included all men, why then did they allow so many black men, women, and children to be hung, beaten, and scorned for what they said (little boys have been lynched for even whistling at a white woman). If they included all men in freedom of religion, why then did they allow our churches to be bombed and our outspoken leaders to be assassinated.

No, they did not intend the constitution for everybody-only for white folks. That is the reason why they pass laws and make new amendments to incorporate many of the people they left out (namely black people). There are unwritten laws for the black man and written laws for the white man. Do you think for one moment that several black policemen could have beaten a white motorist senseless on national t.v. and go to court for it and be found innocent of excessive force (Los Angeles—Rodney King)? White America would have been outraged if they had beaten a dog like that, not to mention a white man. But to them, a black man is less than a dog so they turned their heads as if nothing happened.

They tried the same police officers in another court to see if the motorist's civil rights were violated (what a joke). Before the civil rights trial verdict, they put 600 policemen in ready riot suits and brought out the National Guard. Now do you think for once that they brought all these antiriot men out because they expected justice to be done in court and the jury and judge to be just, or do you think that they already anticipated a fixed trial? I think that they anticipated a fixed trial. I hope that there are no black men stupid enough to think that what has happened to the black motorist and the white policemen in Los Angles does not affect them.

Time and time again black folks have been forced to use the white justice system only to see that white justice means no justice at all.

They had already predicted that by the year 2000 most black families would have single parent's homes and that 90% of our black men will either be in jail or in the grave yard. As I look around me, it appears that they are doing all they can to fulfill this prediction because all that the police does not kill, the judge is putting in jail.

Don't misunderstand me; I think that all crimes should be punished. But the punishment should be across the board-white or black. The murderer should get just as much time for killing a black man as he would for killing a white man. Research shows that the black man gets far more time for killing a white man than those black men killing other black men.

The population of our prisons tells us that we live under a white judicial system. For, in our country black people are a minority. There are about a little above 30 million blacks in the United States as opposed to the over 300 million white folks. Yet in the United States prison system, blacks are the majority. If, in fact, blacks are a minority in the general population, how can they be a vast majority in the prison population; it stands to reason that blacks should be a minority in prison also-seeing that they make up a little over ten percent of the general population.

Marcus Garvey learned first hand of how one sided white justice can be. He was tried and convicted of mail fraud without even a shred of evidence. Up to a point, Garvey believed in the system. Knowing that he would be cleared and the case thrown out of court, Garvey simply represented him self. He soon found out that white justice was not design to acquit black men. They found Garvey guilty and sent him to prison. After his prison term, they extradited Garvey out of the country where he spent his remaining years in obscurity (all this was done because Garvey scared them. He gave them a glimpse of black unity and what it could accomplish if left alone).

They say now that Garvey lost his case because he represented himself (yea, right, and if we believe that, we might as well believe that birds can really fly without wings). Garvey had lost that case even before he set foot in the court room. The white supremist wanted to get rid of him, and fraud through our justice system was the perfect way-and with a little help from an Uncle Tom I might add.

The real reasons why they wanted to get rid of Marcus Garvey is that (1) He was a very intelligent black man. (2) He was a black nationalist; he believed in exaltation and preservation of black people-black enterprise. (3) He was able to positively influence black people to move up (he had over one million followers). (4) He was powerful.

They used their white justice to rid themselves of a black leader who had the capability of changing the destiny of black people everywhere-and he would have done it without a violent revolution.

White justice is so vindictive, so catastrophical until it even eats up its own kind. I recall reading where J. Eager Hoover, the once director of the F.B.I, used the justice system to try and make a known communist (Syrote) talk. Syrote had been found guilty of espionage, but would not give Hoover and his men his contacts. So they came up with this demeaning less than moral plan. They had to some how connect Syrote's Wife to his espionage and then threaten both of them with execution. That way Syrote would talk in order to save his innocent wife (they thought). So without a thread of evidence (just like they did with Marcus Garvey), they arrested Mrs. Syrote also and found her guilty of espionage. Mr. Syrote never talked. They both were executed by electricity while J. Eagar Hoover stood by the phone waiting to hear that Mr. Syrote had stopped the execution of his wife by telling the F.B.I what they wanted to hear.

Two children were left orphans and motherless because the white justice system thought that she was expendable.

The only time white justice will benefit anyone besides the white race is when the white folks will ultimately gain from the results.

For instance, look what happened with Japan. The United States paid restitution to Japan's people who were thrown in concentration camps during the war (regardless if they were United States citizens or not) that our nation had with Japan. The justice system said that the United States paid restitution to those people because locking them up in concentration camps was unlawful.

It seemed as though the United States system of white justice had a conscious-wrong! After weighing the situation, one can clearly see that that restitution movement was merely political. Designed to help build relations between the United States and Japan (at that time, Japan was becoming one of the most powerful and wealthiest nations in the world. They definitely did not want old wounds to get in the way of Japan being one of our economical allies).

I use to wonder when I saw the statue of Liberty, representing freedom and justice, standing there blind folded. But, as I inhale the daily injustices around me, as I swallow the deluded watered down practices of slavery, I now fully understand why the statue that stands for freedom and justice for all is blind folded. They have not exalted pure uninhibited, untampered, justice, and we as a nation have not extended complete freedom to all.

As long as we as a nation stand divided and hypocrites, freedom and justice will always be blind folded and stumble about on the dark paths of inequality with no equilibrium.

HOMICIDE/GENOCIDE

According to research, the leading cause of death among black men, between the ages of 15-45, in the United States is homicide—Usually black men killing black men-black on black crimes. At first glance, it appears that blacks are their own worst enemy.

So often I hear many black men say that we can no longer blame the white man for our troubles because the white man is not the one that is shooting us down-it's us. The white man does not break into our houses-it's us. A black man that makes such a remark is either a fool or he knows very, very little about American history and his environment.

For us to say we can not presently blame the white man is like a doctor experimenting on pigs: He gives them a big dose of L.S.D, then watched the effect it has on them. When the pigs start to fight and kill each other, can't you see the doctors pointing and saying "Look what they are doing to themselves," when in essence, he did it to them.

When we say that we can't blame the white man, it is also equivalent to the researchers test on the effects of cocaine on mice (this test was actually done). They put a vile of cocaine in the mice's cage. After a while the mice wanted nothing but the cocaine-not food, sex, water or even rest, it only wanted cocaine until it died. Now can you not hear the researcher say, "Look at what that mice did to it self for cocaine." When in substance, the researcher killed the mice, and didn't even put a hand on him.

Knowing who to blame for our dismal situation is no excuse for black people to continue on that homicidal, genocidal path. We must become responsible for each other. The question has been asked over and over again down through the channels of history, "Am I my brother's keeper?" Yes, Yes, most definitely. We are responsible for each other and accountable to each other-every time my brother dies, it diminishes me (Earnest Hemingway).

Black homicide is the end result of an enslaved, oppressed, and suppressed people. The only reason why it is black on black is because the only other people he is surrounded by are black people (but if this trend continues, I don't believe that it will remain a black problem because it will migrate).

Black on black crimes are pure untapped angered aggression. Over the years, he had learned to stifle his aggression-but not now.

They say, "But how can you blame the white man for blacks homicidal tendency?" If the white man had not been hypocritical in his endeavors to emancipate the slaves, he would not have legislated laws which he had no intentions of fulfilling "immediately." Emancipation was to take place for the slaves but as they put it, "It had to be a gradual freedom-a little at a time. There in lies the problem; they didn't expect the owners to free the slaves right away-thus, the Bill was passed in 1863 and 1865, but forms of slavery existed even 100 years after they passed the law.

What most people fail to realize is that slavery was an international market. The whole white world was using slaves. They all were feeding off of the dark skinned people of Africa. So, the abolishment of slavery had to be internationally or none at all. Britain abolished slavery as early as 1807 and many other countries followed suit.

The black man had no relief of injustice anywhere. For even though Britain had freed their slaves on paper, in the "natural", black people were still very much still slaves. There were two common situations that followed emancipation: 1) Mr. Charlie would come out of his big house and say to the slaves, "Yalls free now; you can leave if you want." 99% of the time, nobody left; for where would they go? How would they survive? The government had not set aside any form of help for them-so, for Mr. Charlie, it was still business as usual. 2) Mr. Charlie would read the emancipation papers and then totally ignore them-still business as usual.

When the slaves heard about his freedom and ran away, he soon found out that what he thought was freedom, was not freedom at all. As a matter of fact, he was treated even worse. The white world did not look at him as a man, but rather a "use to be" slave.

His anger began to build now, even more than when he was an outright slave. He was already angry from being a slave-watching Mr. Charlie rape his wife when he got ready to, and many times even made her pregnant while, he, the black slave husband, stood outside and listened helplessly. He watched his children be sold and bought like a piece of meat, or a farm animal. So, his anger continued to rise over the years until he could no longer contain.

After emancipation, they whipped him, lynched him, denied him, used and abused him for decades, and now in this present day, they ask why is the black man so homicidal, so aggressive, and so temperamental. I'll tell you why. He is like a steam kettle which has reached its limits and is now about to boil over (but mind you, there is always a mechanism to release some of the steam-as a nation, we just choose not to).

They are not simply asking why because they are concerned that black homicide will eventually assist black genocide. The white supremest are asking why because common sense tells them that it is not long before that black homicide will no longer be secluded to the black neighborhood. It is going to over flow into the white communities.

They will vent their anger at the ones that is responsible for their condition—The ones that has not paid or made restitution; the ones who have walked in the way of their hateful forefathers-the white supremest.

Often times, they say, "Why give me trouble for something that our ancestors did?" There are two reasons why they must bare some blame: 1) they are still walking in their ancestor's footsteps. 2) not only must man account for what he does, but he must also account for that which he fails to do. They fail to make/force a change in the face of injustice.

Over four hundred years of abuse and mental anguish has resulted in the psychological degeneration of a people so completely that they shall never be totally purged of the gross "condition".

No matter how hard blacks try of themselves to get rid of their innate hostile aggression, we cannot without supernatural intervention. Over the years, he have been trained to be aggressive-aggression is a way of adapting, overcoming, and surviving.

As long as there is injustice, there will always be homicide and threatened genocide, but it will not remain only in the black neighborhood-I guess one could say that we learned from the past riots that burning our own neighborhoods didn't make much sense.

The white system continues to increase the black man's anger. Along with all the injustices he puts upon the black man, he continues to psychologically paint a dismal picture of the men in our race. He paints the picture that black men are lazy and don't want to work; that they're just looking for a hand-out. They fail to see (or shall I say don't want to see) the brothers that are working two jobs and doing everything that they can do to provide for their family. But the white supremest is not interested in the blacks who are striving, only the ones who will not work, who sale drugs, and who are just out for themselves.

Every time I look at the news, I see some black man or woman who has been arrested for using or selling drugs. But I wonder why you very rarely see a white man being arrested for using or selling drugs-and they do use and sale it much more than blacks. As a matter of fact, that is where drugs in the black community come from. No matter whose out there selling it; it comes from the white man. How many blacks do you think have ships and airplanes to bring that poison onto our soil?

If they truly want to stop the drug epidemic, they cannot stop at the black pushers or king-pins selling the drug to the black community. They must go across town to the white community and get those white boys whose selling. They must go and get those millionaires whose planes and ships bring it into the United States. They must go into the law enforcement and get those officers who are on the "take" working for the drug dealers. But they cannot stop there; they must travel all the way to capital Hill and get those politicians whose pockets are greased with filthy drug money. Yes, arrest the black man, but also arrest every one else that is involved in the sale and use of drugs. If we dry up the supply, then the demand will inevitably cease.

What is most unfortunate though, is that many of our own black brothers and sister perpetuate the homicide/genocide trend among blacks. In our songs; in our movies we often show case that thug persona of kill or be killed. Rappers rap about thug life; singers sing about thug life. It is no wonder that many of our young men desire to be thugs because those in the entertainment world glorify "thug life". Their mentality is live fast because you won't live long, and take all that you can from anybody that you can. It would be simply wonderful if we had many more rappers with a positive message in their rap, but unfortunately many of them are quite shallow and void of any true substance. Most rap about how long their gold chain is and how much gold they have in their mouth. They rap about their Rolex watches, their diamonds, and their expensive houses and extravagant cars, or how good they are with women-All shallow, empty lyrics. So, the young mind starts to think when he sees the rapper with all of his "stuff", and hears the rapper's lyrics over and over again, it subconsciously ingrains in his thought patterns-you are what you think, and you think what you listen to the most. Why is it that many can learn a rap song verbatim, but cannot maintain a "b" average in school? He knows the lyrics to R. Kelly's song through and through, but he cannot remember his speech at church or school. And some of the entertainers utter, "I am not a role modal." P-lease, by virtue of what he does and the attention that he gets, he is, whether he wants to or not, a role modal. Role modal simply means that some one want to be like you. So, if I could say just one thing to the rappers and singers, it would be, "when you have the mic, please remember some young mind is listening to you and making some decisions on what you say, so say something worth hearing-something that will help accelerate his mind."

It's going to take the entire community to stop the homicide among us. We cannot expect the government to come into our neighborhoods and do what we refuse to do when we live right there. We know who it is doing the "drive bys". Nothing happens without some one knowing. If the president can't stop men from walking up to the White House and shooting at it, what makes us think that he can stop the "drive bys" in our neighborhoods.

EXPLOITATION

We live in a world where exploitation has instinctively become a way of life-a major part of the system. Just as our forefathers were used and exploited, we, the black race, are yet being exploited.

Exploitation in its simplest form means to use someone in a selfish way for gain—in other words, to use someone to exalt ones self. There is no need to expostulate with anyone as to the reason for slavery then or dressed-up slavery now. The bottom line was and still is gain-profit.

From the captains of those slave filled ships to the cotton farmers in Georgia, from the egotistic minds of the murderers who raided African villages, to the fat cats that sit behind big desks on capital him, from the bishops in England, to the preachers on the fertile soils of the United States, from the Africans that sold Africans into slavery, to the black men who helped the white man keep them slaves when they got here, they all used black people for profit. Black people were an international commodity.

I wish that I could stand firm and say that black people have never been exploited by their own. I cannot. For it started in Africa with different tribes selling each other's prisoners of war. Sometimes, they would raid villages for the white man (we still have quite a number of fools who are still raiding our communities for the white man, but only this time it is not to get slaves to sale to the white man, it is to sale drugs to the community for the white man-same results).

There is a grievance in every black man's heart against exploitation today. My people have grown tired of being used and treated like an animal. Many of the problems the U.S. face in the inner cities across the country is due to the drained emotions of an already tired people.

The white system says that the only way that we are going to stop this problem from continuing is that we have got to build bigger jails and hire more policemen. That is like saying lets forget about curing people with cancer, but rather let's build some bigger hospitals and hire more nurses to help ease their pain until they die, or like saying let's not try to cure glaucoma, let's just give them glasses after they go blind. That would be simply ludicrous. It is the same with the bigger prison solution-stupid.

It angers me to see my people being exploited by many of our own leaders. It appears that they are grossly out of touch with the problems facing black people today—the problems that we continue to struggle with daily. Not all of our leaders, but many are using blacks to profit or further their careers in politics or business.

I remember when the blacks in some small county in Georgia had severe racial problems (probably still do). Many black leaders across the country went there to do what they could to better the conditions for the black people living there. But, there were some that exploited the situation and went simply to get media coverage. I recall feeling ashamed when I turned on the news and saw one of our local black leaders on T.V. grinning and smiling while telling the news reporter, "we went to Georgia with a number no man can number." He failed to realize that just having a large number means absolutely nothing if that number cannot produce results of some sort. Just having 30,000,000 black people in the United States does not mean a thing if we cannot come together and make a change.

A march by it self does nothing but bring the attention of outsiders to the plight of the local people. Now, what are you going to do when you get that attention? What kind of plan will you institute after the march is over and the marchers are gone back home? There must be some kind of support after the march. If all one is going to do is march, then one might just as well remain at home (But then I guess you can't be grinning on the news if you remain at home), because just marching does two negative things: 1) It gives those racist a chance to publicly come together and throw racist remarks-stirring up the hate that is already in them. 2) A march by it self only makes conditions worst for those who have to live and remain in that area long after the hype and media is gone.

Exploitation has always been common place in the black community. I remember the experiment done on 399 black men in Tuskegee Alabama. White doctors, who worked for the United States Public Health Service, used them like they were just animals. Having diagnosed syphilis in them, the doctors, did not acknowledge their true diagnosis to their ailing black patients. They simply lied to them and told them that they had some kind of bad blood disease.

They alleged that all this was done so that they could study the effects syphilis has on a man and his off-springs if left untreated. It was not for an adamant desire to create a new drug or new form of treatment for future syphilis patients. It was done merely to see how for this disease could digress-how long it would take to kill its victim, and what kind of shape the victim would be in at the time of death.

This was done for 40 years-1932 to 1972. I personally believe that they were trying to see if syphilis could in some way be used as a biological weapon during war. You might ask yourself how could they do this and get away with it for forty years. This was done in Macon county Alabama. A place that was poverty stricken and shut off from the rest of the world. What we have to understand is that there is no poverty, or slum, or ghetto like the ones that the rural city produces. Because there, they are locked away and shut up from the whole world. No one out side of them seems to care, so they develop this inferiority, low self esteem complex and settle and are content where they are because many of them know no other life-it goes from one generation to another. They are even worst off than the inner city slums and poverty stricken neighborhoods—Because in the inner city, they have other eyes on them. The inner city slum becomes an "eye sore" for the city government. Therefore, they are apt to do something, if not but for "show". So, they will have grants from the federal government and other subsidies trying to help them come out. This does not happen in the rural slums because no one is watching them; if we find out about them, it is only because we happen to stumble upon them, but we soon forget them because they are tucked away-out of sight, out of mind. It is parallel to what some of the cities did in the United States when they were hosting the Olympic Games; they tore down project apartments and built newer ones or just left them down all together. The reason was because they didn't want those "ghettos" to be associated with their city. Do you think that they changed any of the rural slums-no, they were tucked away.

Exploitation at its worst is sacrificing life for their so called science. They tried to exalt themselves with the lives of 399 black men.

I believe for 40 years they tried desperately to harness this disease so that they could use it to their advantage against their enemies. If they could some how harness it and manipulate it to their on purpose, its destructiveness would be immeasurable. You ask why syphilis? 1) They needed a biological weapon that was readily accessible and very lethal that could cause death swiftly. 2) They needed something that had the ability to affect a whole nation. Sex was the key. Everybody is involved in sex. They were not talking about just stopping their enemies, but complete genocide-the enemy and his off-spring.

As outrageous as it may sound, I believe that aids in some way is a direct link from the Tuskegee syphilis experiment. Note, aids and syphilis are contracted the same way. Remember, they were trying to develop a biological weapon that can be spread by way of sex, blood or bodily fluids would have the ability to kill the infected one as well as his seed.

Most would say that is simply impossible. But in 1970, while the experiment of syphilis in Tuskegee was still going on, they offered many house Bills asking for the development of a synthetic biological agent (all of this is public record). They said that it would be possible to produce a synthetic biological agent; an agent that does not naturally exist and for which no natural immunity could have been acquired.

Yes, all of my research points to the analogy that aids was developed in some laboratory. Perhaps it started with some naïve doctor thinking that he was developing something that would help our country become stronger against their enemies, but he failed to realize, like Albert Einstein with the splitting of the atom. Any weapon, whether bomb or biological agent, is only good when it is in good hands. But, when it gets into the hands of men whose minds are twisted, whose thoughts are evil, and whose purpose is death, it becomes a weapon that is not only a threat to our enemies, but a very real threat to the survival of human kind.

A developed weapon such as aids would be a prime consideration for a racist. Imagine what Adolf Hitler would have done with aids as a weapon at his disposal; His killing of the Jews would have far exceeded the millions he's accounted for killing.

By his aids weapon, the racist can wipe out entire black families while he sit somewhere in congress pretending to raise capital for the research of aids.

Some argue that aids was not man made, and that it's not used to kill off black people; and, to give their argument merit, they say that aids is killing just as many white folks as it is black people. The answer to that argument is that aids became a weapon that they could not harness, so it got out of control. The result of that is that while it kills black people, it is also killing white people at an astounding rate. This should not surprise the American people because the government did use biological warfare against the American Indians. They would send diseased blankets and food (infested with small pox) to the Indians and hope that the disease would kill hundreds of Indians-they were successful. Sometimes they would wipe out entire villages of men, women, and children. And, just like aids, some white people, particularly soldiers, died from the disease (small pox) that they transported to the Indian village. The racist simply feels that those "good" white folks died as casualties of a higher purpose-get rid of the Indians.

Hate and racism, which go hand in hand, always kill masses of innocent people besides the ones that they target-even his own kind. We can prove that by the study of Adolf Hitler and Joseph Stalin's lives. They killed many innocent Germans and Russians while trying to rid themselves of those of whom they hated.

The difference between the biological weapons the white man used against the American Indian is that those diseases were controlled by keeping it contained in the Indian villages, but aids cannot be contained or isolated; it spread too fast and jumped racial boundaries. They hadn't thought of the then secret affair between whites and blacks. So, in essence, after they secretly copulated with their infected victims, the white woman and white man, unknown to them, took aids back to their pristine neighborhood, thereby, causing aids to start the kill in unintended communities.

I just believe that aids is the white man's plan gone foul-now, he too is endangered by that which he created. It is quite a paradox; isn't it? If you believe that theory that they produced for the media-aids started in Africa from monkeys, then you ought to go and buy that new beach front property in Idaho-it doesn't exist.

ROCKY ROAD TO FREEDOM

Until we can be absolutely honest with ourselves and face the truth and the facts head-on, no matter what they might reveal, we as a nation will never truly heal the wounds from the past. We must stop lying to ourselves.

Our nation is a growing monster while our leaders tell us that all is well and that we are doing fine. The United States is crumbling little by little and the sad thing is that the masses of the people can't see it-they have no idea.

We are still buying our old slogan, "Land of the free and home of the brave". Wake up! Look at us. While less than five percent of the world's population lives in the United States, we consume more than fifty percent of the world's cocaine. Our national defense budget, which runs in the billions, is equaled by what we spend on alcohol consumption. Fifteen million Americans are diagnosed every year as clinically depressed, and we spend more than five hundred million dollars a year (and climbing) on prescription drugs for antidepressants. All this is amidst considering that the United States is by far the greatest nation in the common world today, and if we are having those problems, just think what the rest of the nations of the world are going through.

When you add it all up, it appears that the American dream is swiftly becoming an American nightmare. The American people spend and enormous amount of time and money to escape reality. And if reality is hard for white America, then it is catastrophic for black America.

If you are still fooled by politicians and think that all is well, then look at the national debt we have. The United States is at present several trillion dollars in debt and it is continuing to grow (by the time this book is published, I am sure that it will have increased by several hundred million). From 1780 until 1965, the debt was 250 billion dollars. In 1980, it was 1 trillion dollars. In 1988, it rose to 2 trillion dollars. In 1994, it was 4 trillion dollars and in 1995, it was well over 5 trillion dollars. Today it is still climbing.

Every world power through out history has had an end but most of them were destroyed by war. If we do not get control of it, this debt will destroy us, or the very least cause us some severe embarrassing moments. After our nation gets so deep in debt, other countries will stop buying our securities-no matter what kind of interest rate we put on their return. Our money shall become worthless. And if foreign countries refuse to accept our money, then that means that we won't be able to purchase enough oil. Without oil, there is no gas, and without gas, there are no trucks to fill our stores and supermarkets. We will still have that worthless money in the bank. If this is allowed to happen, life as we now know it shall be changed. We all shall become barbarians-only the strong will survive. Another country shall have to come in and rule the United States; I suspect it will be China, or Japan, or some other economically rich nation. Now, it ought to be clear to you why the Gulf war and this present Iraqis war took place. Sadaam Huesane played a part, and I believe that he was a threat; the terrorist played a part and I believe that they are a threat that needs to be dealt harshly with, but the real reason for those eastern wars was all about that black gold (oil) which produces green paper (money). For us to say that we're so passionate about the entire world becoming a democratic society, I believe, is a guise to hide their true reasons. If it is truly about forced democracy, why not start with some countries that are a lot closer to us, and perhaps not so dangerous-they don't have oil. This is parallel to when the white man first invaded and colonized Africa. He did it under the guise of religion and he said that he wanted to civilize them. Well, to civilize, means to make civil, to be apart and submit to order of the organized civil authority. The African people already had some type of civil law among them. What the white man meant by civilize, he meant to indoctrinate the African to the American way of life; so their reason for colonizing Africa was for some other undisclosed reason. No, the real reason was they wanted to own those diamond mines, oil, rich minerals, and develop a labor commodity (slavery).

We, as a nation, have got to do something because we are continuing to decline. 14 million people are on welfare in the United States and we spend over 25 billion dollars each year on welfare. Over half of the welfare recipients are teenage mothers. We need to take some of that money and create more jobs to assist some of those people to get off of welfare, and then only the people that truly need welfare will be getting it. Now, we tell them the more babies you have, the more money welfare will pay you. So, the young lady goes and have another baby, or she does not care whether she has one or not, because if she does, her monthly check will increase. On the other hand, there are others that want to work but welfare tells them that if they work, they will lose all of their benefits. They can work, they want to work, but for them, it's not worth it-to get a job that has no benefits, and not enough pay, so, they opt to stay on the system, and I can't say that I much blame them if those are their only options. What we have failed to realize is that welfare was never designed to assist the individual indefinitely; Roosevelt's intentions were to assist them for a time until they are able to get back on their feet. If we reconstruct and change our system, then only the people who truly need welfare will be receiving it and not those who get it because they cannot find a decent job to provide for their family.

Now, amidst all of the debt problems, oil problems, welfare, gas prices, a dwindling dollar, and war, they tell us that social security is running out. One of the very few sources of income the average man has to look forward to because statistics shows that over ninety percent of Americans retire with less than five thousand dollars in the bank. Most are in need of a hand-out from their children or other relative or some other source. Now, you tell them that all that money that the government was taking out of their check is gone-where.

I showed all this so we can truly see where we are. If it is bad for whites, then it is triple for blacks. What is a little drop of rain in their community is a typhoon in the black community.

The fact of the matter is that we are living in a country that is in dire need of reconstruction. So, true liberty will never come for black people as long as we stand with our hands clasped and wait for the government to change things for us. True justice will only come for us by our hands-you and I have got to do for you and I (like the clothing line Fubu-for us by us). Often times, help is right there at the end of your hand.

THE CRY FOR JUSTICE

Africa today possesses the signs of a people invaded by salvages. For many of the people still have the characteristics of their white conquerors who came in the name of religion and civilization. Many of the African people have never left the African continent, but they are still enslaved and influenced by outsiders.

Quite a number of Africa's governments are corrupt and inefficient. Poverty is the common bond between many African people and wealth is the common bond between many African rulers (the people starve to death while the rulers get richer).

North American companies still dominate the economies of many African states, and a number of countries around the world still own most of Africa-especially the wealthy parts.

Some have said for blacks to go back to Africa, and even some blacks have said that we ought to go back to Africa, but that will not solve the problem of injustice or discrimination, and inequality by the white system because the white system owns and operates most of the wealth of Africa. Equality starts right where we are. It all starts with us as individuals. Freedom and equality has always evaded us because we have always readily believed the lie-we are less because we are black. We cannot blame the masses of black people who accepted and adapted to the white man's psychological image of them because the lie was delivered with such cunning until even Satan himself is probably amazed.

All through his life, the black man has been drilled on how good "white" is. Consider the story of Santa Clause. Some white man dressed up in a red suit, driving a magical sleigh with flying reindeers, is going all over the world giving toys and gifts to children—particularly underprivileged black children. It is remarkable how black people, knowing that it is a lie, will continue to teach their children as they were taught about this generous white man in a red suit.

Look at what old Santa Clause does. Mama and daddy, who have worked hard and denied themselves so that they can get their children something for Christmas, give all their credit to the white man in the red suit. So, when little Johnny wakes up and sees all of his gifts, he does not thank Mama and Daddy. He thanks the white man, Santa Clause, for what he has. And you can't blame him because Mama and daddy told him, "Santa Clause brought you that." What that tells Johnny psychologically is that if you be good, the white man will take care of you and give you nice things. He can't even thank God on Jesus birthday for thanking the white man in the red suit-Santa Clause. It's really sacrilege, anti God. They have made a god out of this Santa Clause. Look what the characteristics are of Santa. He knows everything-whether you are bad or good (sounds like God doesn't it); He goes all over the entire earth in one night, and he rewards those that have been good.

In every aspect of his life, until he opens his minds eye and awake, the black man has been taught that white is good and that black is bad. Look at how they present Jesus. He was a Jew. He grew up in Israel, one of the hottest places on earth and yet when we see supposedly pictures of Jesus, he does not have olive skin like most living in that region, but rather, the picture that they paint of Jesus is white. Do you think for a moment that they were not aware that he was a Jew, and that he was born and raised in Israel? They had to make Jesus look like them, thereby; psychologically perpetuating the mind set that white is "good".

Black people can never move up until we change the image that the white system has given us. We must tell our children the truth so that they and their children will walk in the light of truth.

They can never silence the cry for justice. Fire could not do it; bullets could not do it; hangings could not do it, and even death and the grave could not silence the cry for justice. The racist burned our houses, shot our leaders, hanged our brave men and caused a multitude of gallant men who cried for justice to go to an early grave. Never-the-less, the victims of injustice keep on crying.

There have been many great black men to rise up out of our people and stand for the masses of mistreated blacks. Among them is a number of whom I must expound upon:

Martin Luther King: King was one of the greatest and most loved black leaders of our times. King was a man of higher learning. Through his methods of non violence, he changed our nation's mistreatment of black people. It was pure genius the way Dr. King organized his marches and used the white system to further his cause. Some folks get lost trying to immolate the marches, but the march was not what brought about a change. Change came because during his marches, Dr. King used the white man's T.V cameras and photo news. Every time the racist did something to the marchers, it was shown on T.V, or seen on the news paper's front page. And whether white or black, nobody wants their ugly closet skeletons shown to the world.

Dr. King knew that the media would show the white man his ugly side, the side he tries to keep hidden. All through the years, the white man had been lying to himself about how good he was, but really deep down inside he knew that he was a beast that fed on the pain, suffering, and fear of the helpless. Most of the ugly things the racist did, he did it under the pretense of religion. Dr. King simply brought the racist face to face with his true identity-a greedy, uncompassionate, hateful, ruthless, merciless, salvage.

When he saw himself beating little children and dragging blooded women and men down the streets, when he saw himself putting vicious dogs on innocent people, he thought to himself, "no that can't be us "good" white folks."

Dr. King shed the last drops of his blood for his people. He cried for civil rights for black people. He wanted the white man to honor the laws and amendments he had made to the constitution. The 13th amendment freed the black man; the 14th amendment made him a citizen, and the 15th amendment gave him the right to vote. During

King's march, the white man already had passed a civil rights bill; he just was not acknowledging it.

Dr. King, during his short life, tried to liberate his people. I thank God for Ralph Abernathy's book "And the Walls came tumbling down". Although many black leaders discouraged a lot of people from reading it, it is a book that needs to be read by every black person.

After reading Abernathy's book, for the first time, I felt like I really knew Dr. Martin Luther King Junior. I have much more respect for him as a man and the work that he did; for in reading the book, I see that he was a man with such passions as I have, with fears as I have and who faced continued disappointments as I have. I honor him the more because with all of his humanly frail characteristics, he still led a multitude of suffering people to freedom and got the white man to change some of his ways.

Malcolm X: Unlike Dr. King, Malcolm was not a man who had acquired a great degree of official higher learning. Through reading and self studying, Malcolm became one of the most articulate and stirring orators of the 20th century. Malcolm's life shows us that it does not matter where you are from, but where your mind is now, or where you've been, but where you're going. And it does not even matter what you've done, but rather what you are presently doing.

It has been several decades since Malcolm's assassination, and many years since his voice echoed for justice, and yet people, black and white, still don't realize the profound impact he had on America. He was aggressive, intelligent, and militant. White folks called him militant because he was outspoken. When the white man says what is on his mind, they call him just outspoken, but when the black man says what is on his mind, the white man calls him militant.

He convinced many black people to believe in themselves and not to just sit back and take what ever the white system tried to do to them. Malcolm taught us that we too have a right to life. He said to acquire this right to life; we must be willing to get it "by any means necessary".

They said that he did not mean violence and that he was speaking from a political point of view. But, having studied Malcolm's life, in his statement, he meant violence if nothing else.

He was years ahead of his times; for while everyone else was crying civil rights, Malcolm cried for human rights. Malcolm knew that as long as we cried for civil rights, our problem would remain just a United States problem. So, he began to preach for human rights. And, if our problem is human rather than civil, then the League of Nations as well as the whole world would be involved.

While I deeply admired Dr. Martin Luther King's nonviolent civil rights movement, I must agree with Malcolm. How can you have civil rights when you are not treated as a human being? Because he was going to make our problem an international problem, they had to have him assassinated. I say they because although some Muslim brothers pulled the trigger, I believe someone in high government organized it (I believe the same person had King, Malcolm, John and Robert Kennedy killed; the killer was in high government, and the only one that would gain the most by all of their deaths). They capitalized on the growing tension between Malcolm and the Nation of Islam.

Most remember him as Malcolm X, and I suppose that is what the white racist would want us to only remember. To truly understand Malcolm, you've got to look at the last phase of his life when he changed his name to Shabazz after coming back from Mecca. As Malcolm X, he was full of hate and revenge. He thought that all white men were devils. As Shabazz, he was full of love for all men, but still wanted justice for his people. He learned that all white men are not evil.

If we are to immolate him, let us try to be more like the Malcolm X that evolved into Shabazz (all men are brothers).

Lewis Farrakhan: Farrakhan was one of the many contemporary black leaders trying to speak out for justice for the black race. Some time ago the government started an investigation on Farrakhan. They said that he had something to do with Malcolm X assassination...Everybody knows that they cared nothing about Malcolm then or now, and they certainly don't want justice; so why would they investigate Mr. Farrakhan—to stop him by tarnishing his character. They feel that any black man with as much power as Farrakhan had was a danger to the white system. What they tried to do to Farrakhan, they did and succeeded with Marcus Garvey (tried and sentence without any evidence).

I chuckled when I saw on the news some time ago where the white congressmen were trying to change their own laws to satisfy themselves. They have the law freedom of speech, but when one of Farrakhan's lieutenants used that freedom to say abrasive things about white folks and other nationalities (I didn't agree with him, but "rights" have to be equal across the board), they came together and tried to change their laws to silence him. How hypocritical. Not once have I seen or heard them meeting to change the freedom of speech law to stop some of the slanders they put upon black people-never heard of them trying to form an amendment against black people being called nigger.

As long as there is injustice, God will always send us gallant leaders to cry for us in the light of liberty.

THE INDIANS TAUGHT US

No race of people has ever been as humiliated, mistreated, slaughtered, and enslaved as the American Indians. The Indians were a peaceful people. They just wanted to live in harmony with the land and man. So when these water people (what the Indians first called the white explorers because they came off of the water) came, they accepted them expecting to share everything. When the Indians told the first explorers that the land did not belong to anyone, that was all the white man needed to hear. For all the land he did not trick the Indian out of, he simply took by force-90% of it he took by force, even the land that the Indians lived on.

Had the Indians known the treachery of the white man, he would have fought with tooth and nail to stop the white man from landing on their soil. The Indian soon found out that the white man did not want to share the land. He wanted all the land for himself. And by the time the Indians decided to fight back, it was far too late. Before the Indians could organize and form a strong offence, the white man had destroyed hundreds of tribes and killed many thousands of Indian warriors. Sometimes they would go in and kill an entire village of men, women, and children-and they called the Indians salvages.

Most would like to believe that somebody else did this, but the United States government's blue coat army hunted them down like animals. Not because they were a threat, but simply because the government did not want any future Indian revenge.

All the Indians that the United States did not slaughter, they made them move to some barren land where few things grew called a reservation. The only thing the white man hated more than black people during those days were Indians-at that time blacks posed no real problem.

The real tragedy behind it all is that the Indians (the few that's left) are at present still on the reservation where life is almost unbelievable. In the land that we call plenty, the Indians are living in poverty and starving to death right now.

The white system is still about its hypocritical ways. I saw on the news where they had opened up a museum of ancient Indian artifacts in New York. I suppose that it is a place where little white boys and girls can go and gasp as they see real Indian pottery, and real Indian moccasins, and real Indian bows and arrows. They gasp and think that these artifacts are from Indians dead and gone, not realizing that those Indians are tucked away in Arizona on the reservation wearing worn out shoes (not moccasins), eating from dirty pots, and living in shack houses, and if they have bows and arrows, there is little to kill on that barren land. The white man said that they put this museum up to honor the American Indian. I thought that if they really want to

The only promise that the white man kept with the Indian

……….I WILL TAKE YOUR LAND………

……….AND HE DID…………

Honor them, then go to the reservation camp and make life better for the Indians there.

The black race can look at the American Indian and see that if we leave our fate in the hands of the white system, we too shall end up on some reservation or worst.

They have not tried to rectify conditions with the Indians because they keep the Indians out of sight-out of sight, out of mind. Some will suggest that things have changed, but I still see the white system propelling itself for more power. I watch them devour our president that the people selected. They are always doing a "witch hunt", trying to find anything that might destroy him so that they can have some of that power. It has been said that when dogs have no other prey to hunt, they will turn on themselves and eat each other-so I guess their actions speak for it self.

We should always keep the Indians in mind—In doing so, hopefully, we will not make the same mistakes that they made.

FALLEN HEROES

No matter how famous and how rich black men become, they still suffer from the pains of racism. It appears that sooner or later the white system shows us that we cannot now nor ever will truly escape racism. All of those blacks who ascend to greatness that the black community is proud of and looks up to, the white system systematically tries to tare up their character.

It angered me to see how they treated Michael Jackson. All of his money and fame and fans could not stop the California district attorney from inhumanely using Michael. They treated him like he was an animal-like he was only 3/5 human. That is how America felt about Negroes in 1600-1865. I do believe that everyone should pay for crimes of which they have committed, but I thought, for some crazy reason, that we are all innocent until proven guilty. Do you think for one moment that any white entertainer of Michael Jackson's magnitude would have had to pull down his or her pants to prove their innocents? The message they sent to Michael and the rest of us is, "We don't care how much money you have or how great you become, to us, you are still just a nigger!"

When I watched and read about the trial of Mike Tyson, I was simply flabbergasted when I heard their verdict of guilty. The law states that in order for one to be found guilty there has to be no reasonable doubt. Look at the evidence. She goes to his place at 2am in the morning with her P.Js on. Somewhere during that time, she said Mike approached her for sex. After refusing him several times, she said that she went in the bathroom and pulled off her panty liner. There was a phone on the wall in the bathroom, but she never called for help. Now what other reason would you go and pull off your panty liner except that you are anticipating sex. The witnesses that could prove Mike's innocents, the judge did not allow them to testify. If one looks at all the events surrounding the case, Mike Tyson was found guilty even before the trial began-make an example out of him.

Now we see the same thing happening to Bill Cosby, but the only thing about Bill, which I admire, is he is willing, able, and ready to fight. Bill Cosby had no problems until he decided to help his people-to go around the country making speeches about how we need to better ourselves and our children. He had no problems until he said that he didn't care what the white man said about him. Now, they are attacking his character. All these women are coming out of the closet saying that Cosby molested them. One of them said that it happened over ten years ago. They have just found some money hungry women to come forth to help them put Cosby in his place. I pray that he makes it through all of this.

The white man has always used the media to fool the people. I watched them use the media to try and diminish Michael Jordon's popularity among the people. Jordon, loved by both black and white, character discussed them. Here is a black man who has money, fame, and who is also a family man. They searched and searched to find something to dishonor and discredit him. The only thing that they could find was his desire to gamble. They stretched gambling as for as they could. They tried to make him out to be such an addict at gambling-that failed. Now I am waiting to see what else will they come up with to try and make him look bad in our eyes. They probably won't do anything else now that he has retired, because they feel that he is no longer an image that makes our sons dream positively-he is a fading image. Jordan won't have any more problems with them if he keeps his voice silent and don't speak out on the issues that's plaguing his people. But, if he does not, they will find something-they always do, and they don't need a "smoking gun".

The white law makers would have never treated Elvis the way that they treated James Brown. Sent to prison for shooting up his office building and failing to stop for the police. Sure, his actions warranted the law to do something, but the way they treated him was like taking a jack hammer to kill a nat. When they were able to flash across the T.V,

"James Brown, the god father of soul, has been sentence to prison." They had achieved their purpose-kill his image and his character, and those that will want to aspire to be like him will desist, or at the very least, decrease.

It just happen by chance that Mohamed Ali's number for the army draft came up when he was at the peak of his career-or did it. The government, knowing full well that Ali would probably respond the way he did, was ready to strip him of his title and freedom (they did the very same thing to Jack Johnson). You say why Ali? Well, because for them, Ali sent the wrong message to the black community. He was young, militant, outspoken, and unafraid. His message to the black race was for them not to be afraid of the white system, and to stand up for what they believed in-freedom and justice for all. As Jack Johnson was, Ali seems to not care about how white people felt about him. And on top of all that, he was a Muslim that taught black enterprise, and black pride in self.

They couldn't find a great white hope to beat him, so they did it with the pen. These days are often referred to as dressed-up slavery. Now, instead of out right hanging you with a rope, they hang you with a pen. Instead of sending the Klu Klux Klan to your house at night to drag you out in front of your family, now they send police men to kick your door down and drag you out in front of your family—How else could you explain kicking the door down on several members of the "black panther" party, or even now, all the black men shot down by the police for nothing. In New York, a black man was shot several times by the police; he had no gun. When the police was asked why they shot him, they said that he went for his wallet and they thought that he was going for a gun. When they killed the panthers, they ran in with a barrage of bullets-killing most of the black men in the house, and mind you, they were in bed-killed before they could even rise up.

They couldn't just kill Ali; he was too popular with the people. They tried to stop him without killing him-it failed. Instead, they gave Ali a greater platform by which to speak.

They marked their own law of entrapment so that they could destroy Mayor Marion Barry. What Mayor Barry was doing was wrong. If they had waited, sooner or later, they would have caught him in his crack addicted habit. But, they could not wait; they went and hired his ex-girlfriend to lure him into a hotel where they had already set up cameras to film him in the very act of smoking crack while in an adulterous affair. Because it was so obvious that they had set him up, the people, after they had stripped him of mayor and humiliated him in front of the entire nation, made him mayor again. I guess the citizens of that city figure that if they could do this to one of the highest ranking black official, then those below him didn't stand a chance. So, the citizens showed their disapproval of the city's wicked shenanigans; they fought and won at the ballot box. I can just imagine that them flaunting their political power made those racist turn colors.

The afore mentioned men are men who have had criminal charges and accusations brought against them. So, some will say that what happened to them is justified. But, what about those who have no charges against them, like the many black mayors and political figures across the nation, but the white system is always on a "witch hunt" trying to find what ever damaging information they can find-and you know that when it comes to investigating most of us, we all have some unfavorable past that we're not particularly proud to share with others.

No matter how much they try and destroy our heroes, we will keep on looking up. We shall stand unshaken in our beliefs that "right" will prevail over "wrong" until our change come-so try as they might to destroy us, we shall not be moved.

OUR SOLUTION

Many books have gone down in history as stating the problems, but we know the problem, for we live in it daily. We want to manifest not only the problems, but the solutions as well.

The black race carries the solution to their problems right in their bosom. Our hearts have got to change, and most importantly, we have got to change our mentality.

The reason why change does not occur in many of us is because we still carry the same heart and the same mind which we have always had. That is why most will physically leave the ghetto, but unfortunately, they will take the ghetto with them in their hearts and mind. You see, it is alright to live in the ghetto because sometimes we can't control our situation, but don't let the ghetto get inside of you.

Often times you will see many young singers and rappers who make it big and earn lots of money, but they still act the way they did when they were in the ghetto and had to fight to survive. They are that way because they never stopped to change their hearts and mentality.

The heart of a man is his spirit-the part of him that makes him who he is, unique and different from all others. The heart is what makes some men fail and other men succeed. His heart is his determination; his drive and strive to accomplish the task at hand. The heart feeds man's mentality. That is why men who have no heart have low mentalities, or shall I say their mentality equals their hearts. Men with no heart usually compromise their character; lose their integrity, live in fear, and settles for whatever is dished out to them. They are the ones that say things like, "just go alone for peace sake. Don't make any waves, things going to change one day."

I have had the privilege to watch a horse be broken. They do it by first capturing a wild horse that is use to freedom and running wild. He is placed in a corral where he keeps running and prancing, trying to find freedom. He cannot be rode or controlled because he is still full of heart. In order to break his heart, first they don't feed him, then they strap themselves to him and ride him until he is tired, run down and can resist no longer (sounds familiar-huh). After taking away his heart, they ride him as long as they like and lead him where ever they want without him even lifting one hoof to resist.

Now look at it from the black man's perspective. After the slave traders first captured them. They kept them locked up in chains. When the slave got to their owners, the first thing the owners did was change the slave's name. The masters gave the slaves his name. He would whip him and whip him until the slave learned to answer by his new name. All this was done to systematically take away his heart. So, thereby, his mentality changed from African free man to American slave.

Now, many generations later, the black man still has not fully regained his heart. Because of that, many of my brothers and sisters retain the enhanced mentality of a slave. That's why many of us are materialistic, selfish, and unable to trust even those that are closes to us.

Many will protest this analogy and say that there is no way that we can now, generations later, suffer mentally from the scars of slavery. Well, look at one of God's lower animals who don't have the mental capacity of humans, but still suffer from something that was done to them hundreds of years ago. Observe the penguin; here is a bird that has wings, but can't fly or shall I say he has mentally blocked out flying...He's a bird, but he swims like a fish; why, because long ago one generation of penguins stopped flying as much and started diving for food. With each succeeding generations, they flew less and swam more until one generation did not fly at all. It was instinctively drawn to the sea.

That's what has happened to the black race. They have learned all to well how to disrespect themselves, how to be disloyal to each other, how to think of themselves as less than others, and how to hate one another, or how else can we logically explain the escalating black on black crimes

We as a people must change. We must recapture the heart (determination, zeal, drive) that our forefathers had prior to slavery. The white man had painted the picture of Africa's people as being wild and bar-

barian and that Africa, the mother land, is simply a jungle. He does this because he does not want blacks to realize their rich heritage. The African people were and are one of the first and most advanced people of the world. I did not say the most civilized because civilized simply means to be able to be governed by a higher authority—rules and regulations. So, there was no question that they were civilized. They were highly advance. If you don't believe it, do some research on that part of Africa called Egypt or Ethiopia.

If the black race can recapture their hearts like Chaka Zulu-a Zulu king in central Africa who fought the British soldiers so hard until for the first time the white man thought about leaving Africa, or recapture their heart like an African warrior named Witbooli; at 80 years old, he was still fighting in the war for freedom; Witbooli fought until the last drop of his blood was spilled for freedom in the Congo. Most men at 80 are thinking of retiring, or accepting the way things are, but not Witbooli; his last day was for the cause of freedom. Or like many of the unsung heroes in our towns across the nation; some of them fighting alone because everybody else is afraid to fight the system,

What most of us do not realize is that we are going to stand for something or die for nothing; we are a part of the solution, or a part of the problem.

So, the very first thing that the black race must do is recapture their hearts and change their mentality. That is truly the first step towards liberation. Secondly, we've got to train our children. We cannot afford to sit back and hope that the white man will teach them right—Child training begins at home.......We cannot afford to sit back and hope that the white man will teach them right—Child training begins at home. We cannot expect anyone else to take time for our children if we don't. It is not the public school's responsibility to teach the black child his heritage. Even the schools that are predominantly black, teach very little black heritage. They are too busy trying to give those youths white minds. Yes, they need algebra, English, and all that other learning which adds to or builds on to their being. But, a black man, without a firm grasp on who he is, will never reach his peak of excellence—no matter how much learning he acquires. It is like building a beautiful home on a weak foundation. When we teach them who they are, they will never have to suffer from the pain of an inferiority complex.

Desegregation hurt us almost as much as it helped us. I am fully aware that because of desegregation we have black doctors, lawyers, and other black professionals that would not have been other wise. Because of desegregation, our children have the Opportunity to attend white schools which have the best learning equipment. But while attending the white schools, they also have the misfortune of associating with and observing derelicts, dissidents, and rebels who would stand in the teacher's face, while the class watched, and call her names which are unmentionable even in private. Knowing full well that little or nothing would be done to him, their actions toward the teacher gets worst. Our children did not do such things because we were taught better-our teachers whipped us, and when we got home, our parents whipped us because the teacher had to. So, now the black students are immolating the white students and are becoming as much a rebel at school as the white kid.

We need to start our own schools and the quality of our education must not be inferior to any other school. We must not allow our schools to become battle grounds, or havens for criminal actions, or even still, a place that is full of drugs. Our children must learn morals at home and come to school to learn how to develop their minds.

Education must be a requirement. I am not talking about just going to school and finishing; many students finish school and can't even read a simple book—and I don't believe in letting them march on graduation day with the rest of the students when they don't have enough credits to graduate. I saw some black parents on T.V. arguing because the school was not going to allow their children to march until they finished their requirements. I could not believe it; they were actually mad because their child could not just march and pretend to graduate with the rest of the class. They should have been angry with the school system if they had not taught their child, or even more so (which is usually the problem) angry with their child for not getting his lessons, and finishing the required classes. No, they were angry because everybody would know that their child didn't graduate-so give him a piece of paper and let him march across stage pretending.

Today, 92% of white children are literate, whereas, with black children, 58% is only literate. In Rochester, New York, out of 700 black high school graduates in 1985, only 23 had a "B" average or better. In California in 1983, out of 24,000 blacks that graduated from high school, only 838 met the requirements to enter the University of California. So, research proves that just going to school and finishing is not enough

The problem in the black community is that we so often send our children off to school and don't worry about them until they arrive home in the evening. In order for us to produce positive change in our black youths lives, and enhance their learning capabilities, we, the black parents and guardians, must step up to the plate, and be there for our children. You ought to know what kind of grades your child is going to have on their quarterly report card even before it comes home; that means that you got to help them with their home work, or get someone who can. You have got to meet with their teachers frequently, and let them see your face at P.T.A meetings, ball games, and other school functions. We can't blame the teacher if we are not doing our part. We've got to show the teachers that we support them while they are trying to give our children a good education. Make sure that she is not having a problem out of your child before you go and want to curse the teacher out. When a complaint comes home from the school about your child, 85% of your response should be on the teacher's side until you learn differently. They can't fight your child and teach them at the very same time; that's why I believe in zero tolerance in schools-if your child doesn't want to learn, the schools should not allow them to disrupt and stop the students who are applying themselves and trying to learn.

As much as I want prayer in the schools, I am not overly concerned if they don't allow prayer in school. School is a place designed to teach academics to young minds. Education teaches our children to think quickly and how to solve difficult problems; that is what it is suppose to do, and if it teaches our children moral, character, and discipline along the way, then I am thrilled. Some of the complainers are crying about no prayer at school, when they should be crying first about no prayer at home. Don't expect the teacher to do that which you refuse to do.

If we ensure that they get a good education, we can change the world one graduate at a time. Why do you think that the white man did not want the slave to learn to read and write? When the white man sees an educated black man, to him, that means one thing-he is a thinker, and if he is a thinker then maybe he is a dreamer. And any black man who has a grasp on who he is, who thinks and dreams, is always a threat to the white system.

We must also put a reverence of God in our children as early as possible; for they can be highly educated, know their heritage, and have a good sense of self worth, but they will never truly fulfill themselves until they have a relationship with their creator. The creature must know the creator. We have got to fill our Sunday's schools and worship services with our children. Sometimes it makes me feel good to hear the voice of a baby in our worship service; for it reminds me of the church of tomorrow and those that will carry the torch to another generation.

We have got to address our ills and problems. We can no longer afford to act like they don't exist, or that they will go away by themselves. With such a mentality as "things will work themselves out", our return back to complete slavery is inevitable.

We have got to face the issue of injustice and bring it to the light. It does my heart good to hear some of the rappers and singers addressing the issues in their music and not talking so much about how big his house is, or how much bling bling he has. Because our youths are musically inclined, music should be one of the methods used to awaken them. I have heard a number of preachers get up in their pulpits and say that rap music is nothing but occult. They obviously had not taken the time to listen to some of the lyrics in many of our rappers songs. They are simply responding like most white Americans-when they find something that they don't understand or know, they try to kill it or enslave it. If rap is going to help pull our young brothers and sisters up, and raise their mentality, then I am all for it. I just wish that they would use less profanity-that's my personal preference. I am of the persuasion of Malcolm X when it comes to saving our youth-by any means necessary.

I solute the many brothers and sisters who are trying to send a message to our black race through their music; such as Ice Cube, Arrested Development, and of course the late great Bob Molly who was one of the pioneers of sending a message in the music. The list goes on and on of brothers and sisters trying to send a message of hope and encouragement to the black race.

Everywhere black people turn; they must be forced to face the issues and the facts of injustice. Because we like going to the movies and watching T.V, we must address the issues of false equality and injustice in those places as well. Spike Lee and John Singleton are doing a great job in their movies showing us that we need to wake-up. But, we need more brothers and sisters to become more involved—many of them don't want to risk losing their status in Holly Wood.

Our brothers who are in positions of fame must take a stand as Arsenio Hall did—show the white man that all of his money can't by some of us. As long as Arsenio was making them laugh and acting foolishly, he could say almost anything, act any kind of way, but as soon as he decided to bring someone on his show that was not clowning, who could shake the black sleeping giant, they told him no, he could not bring that kind of person on the show. He wanted to bring Louis Farrakhan on the show to expound upon his views. They told him if he did, they would cancel his show. He still brought Farrakhan, and they kept their word also-they cancelled his show.

I can imagine that it really shook them up to see a young black comedian with far more in him than jokes. Arsenio had the means to address the issue, so he chose Farrakhan to speak, and none can speak on the issues of injustice, and racial disparity as Farrakhan could.

When we speak of great men standing up for what they believe in, and willing to risk everything, let us not forget our brother Arsenio Hall.

If we are to achieve, we must face the issues—In doing so, our perspective of the dismal situation as a whole will change.

In order to change this perpetual state of inequality and injustice, we must pool our strengths-economically, politically, and socially. When we study the history of all the great empires, we find that they all had one thing in common when they were destroyed. The enemy always capitalized on their division. The Aztec, Roman, Persian, Greece, and many many others were all destroyed because they were divided.

Consider the Indians; the primary cause of their defeat was their lack of unity. The Spanish explorer, Cortes, conquered the Aztec Indians of Mexico with just a few men. Not because they were fearful, but because they were divided and Cortes capitalized upon that. He got the Indians to start fighting each other (sounds familiar-huh).

We have got to pool our strengths and strengthen our weaknesses. Black people account for hundreds of millions of dollars each year in the United States economy. We add to the growth and strength of America. We are the second largest race in the United States, and yet we are denied life, liberty, and the pursuit of happiness more than any other ethnic group.

To make it plain, any business that our money supports, we are able to make some changes in it. If we give IBM a large percentage of their business, then we ought to go tell them these are the changes you must make in your company-such as more black managers. If we buy more cadilacs than anybody else, then we ought to go to general motors and make some changes. Tell them to make agreeable changes, or blacks will not buy their cars. They will make the changes because the white man loves green more than he hates black.

After we pool our economical strength, we must come together socially. We must realize that directly and indirectly we are affected by everything that happens to any one of us. We must protect our neighborhoods and keep our communities clean. We must stop buying stolen goods because if they can't sell it, they will stop steeling it; that alone will have an impact on house burglary.

If we, as a black race, ever realize how much strength we truly have, we will no longer just look for a hand out, but we will demand some changes right now. For instance, we are the second largest group of people in the U.S, and because of that, we play a large role in who becomes our next president. No man can win the election without our vote-at least a large part of our votes. Now, if he needs us to win, why not put our agendas on his table. If he wants our votes, he has to address our issues. When he starts campaigning, we must start campaigning. We must collectively decide what issues are plaguing the black community. Those sound good speeches are fine, but I am interested in what is he going to do when he stops tickling our ears and steps away from the podium. When he goes into the oval office, are our issues at least on his desk with other "things to do" projects.

If we follow the afore mentioned plans, we can change the "slavery to slavery syndrome. It will be from slavery to freedom-as it ought to be.

SPECIAL NOTE

If we are to change our condition, we've got to change our social life. Women and men have got to change their behavior towards each other. The reason why so many of our children become trouble stricken is because they're from dysfunctional families. Mothers and fathers are still living according to the slave plight-they are against one another; they are together by force.

The black man as a slave was simply a breeder. He went from house to house impregnating the black slave women. He had no ties, no responsibility towards the woman or the children. Some of the slaves even boasted about being a breeder and how many children they had.

Because of the male's breeding duties, he was unstable and unpredictable. So, the black woman assumed both mother and father position with the children. And even during the few times that the father tried to remain with his family, his role as a father was a weak one at best-to say the least. The slave women were conditioned to discourage any aggressive behavior in black men; wherefore, when he came to her, he oftentimes felt worst about his situation, even to the point that it was his own fault that he was in the condition that he was in.

We are suffering socially today from those learned behaviors. Like breeders, our black men, young and old, are going from one woman to another impregnating them as they go. He refuses any ties and shuns all responsibilities. If he takes care of the children, the court has to force him. The white slave master raised his children then, and now, the white man is still raising his children today-they call it welfare.

The black women still plays the dominant role in the family. She continues to maintain that role, but shows hostility towards her mate because she does. To ease her conscious, she says, "Well, somebody has to lead this family." Because of this, one of the most consistent characteristics of the husband and father is subdued authority that is controlled by the wishes and whims of his wife-Laymen call this condition "henpeck".

What-so-ever we see abroad comes from home—Many of our down-falls, we have nurtured and cherished through the years. In order to lift ourselves to a higher and more successful level, we must abandon our prior behaviors which the white man forced upon us.

We must teach our sons to be faithful to his mate, and if he can't take care of the child, don't have the child. With sex, come responsibilities. When a child is conceived, it took two people to do so; it also takes two to raise the child. The child needs his father as much as he needs his mother; a woman cannot, by herself, teach a boy how to become a man. We have got to teach our young brothers that there is nothing honorable about sleeping with more than one woman. It's a disgrace. They are just keeping the tradition that the slave master taught them-stop being a slave.

Women have got to start encouraging their men; stop reinforcing what the world says about him (that he is no good). If he is not the leader of the home, help him become the leader he needs to be. Give him no other choice. That means that the woman has to become submissive and supportive to her man.

God never intended for the woman to lead the family. The world tells him that he is nothing; she should make him feel like he is everything. But if he refuses to be faithful, she should not tolerate it at all—get rid of him. Every sister that knows that her mate is being unfaithful and puts-up with it is adding to the problem of breaking the slave mentality that many of our black men have.

The black man must be everything to the black woman, and the black woman must be everything to the black man-we must rebuild each other.

BEHOLD, HOW GOOD AND HOW PLEASANT IT IS FOR
BROTHERS TO DWELL TOGETHER
IN UNITY

PSALM 133:1

"UNITY"

SYNOPIC

Too often, we try to categorize our creator, the supreme being-God. We make him Baptist, Lutheran, Methodist, Muslim, Catholic, Hindu, and a host of others. Man, as such, has always tried to categorize, or shall we say "contain" God.

God is far too deep for any or all of us to contain or even categorize. He is just too deep. It is like trying to grasp the ocean. It is far too deep to even understand; all that we know of it and many of the things that it contains, we still know only very little about the ocean-so is man with God. It's like walking to the beach and dipping up a glass full of ocean water and thinking that you have the ocean in your glass-so it is with these modern day God "people" (they have their own knowledge of god-fixed or real). They acquire a little knowledge of him, and then proclaim that they know him. But in essence, they only know of him; for to truly know him is to understand that you don't know him and that one will never fully know God until he is one with God-thus, the paradox. The only way that anyone can be one with their creator completely is through death; anything else is parallel to the dip in the ocean; to become "one" with the ocean and all of its mystery, one must drown-and even then, you are still not one with the vast ocean; you would simply be a shell floating "in" the ocean.

I am often amazed at how man, with all of his frailties, try to scale God down; that is why their religion is like diluted unsweetened tea—while it can quench your thirst, you will never ever enjoy rich flavor, or true quality. With all of their preaching, charity, praising, and song, they still don't know the father. Because of this vast gulf between god and man, to fulfill himself, man, play acts his religious experience, or gave divine purpose and birth to some object he designed to worship.

Poverty and distress have always compelled man to seek his creator; riches, wealth, and gain with no wisdom push man away from him. But, I've notice among both, the rich and the poor; they all want to make God their errand boy. The poor says," Come deliver us" and the rich says, "Give us more." It is no wonder then why Adolph Hitler said that religion is the opium of the masses. Religion is where we all meet—the rich, the poor, the wise, and the fool; they all meet at religion and most leave with a perplexed sense of who and what god is.

Most Christians miss the point of Jesus; they seem to believe that Jesus came for them to worship him, so thus they pray to Jesus, and their relationship is only with Jesus. That's not what Jesus came for. He came to rebuild our relationship with the father; that's why he made all of his children priests.

By large Christianity the religion has cast a shadow over the gospel. I suppose that before we journey any further in this application, I deem it of necessity to clarify the term Christian, or Christianity. The bible affirms that the Apostles were first called Christians at Antioch. Then, the term meant men who act just like Jesus the Christ. So, the "bible" does not say that does who believe in Jesus are Christians, but rather a sect of people called Jesus' followers Christians. Seemingly they would have called them Jesusian, after his name rather than his title. His name was Jesus; his title was Christ—meaning Messiah—and, that is what "messes" them up-thinking that they are little messiahs is the delusion that has inextricably destroyed their knowledge of the "fullness" of god.

All through history white America and Europe cast a dark shadow over Christianity. They did Jesus a great disservice-they discredited his name, title, and purpose. If one was to try and understand just who Jesus was by observing the Christians of past and present, one would have to conclude that Jesus was greedy, mean, hateful, vengeful, and full of malice. We know that that would be a lie, and that Jesus was quite the opposite. But, by the same token too, Jesus was no sissy in a long white robe with soft frail skin. Jesus was a militant radical teacher during his life.

Most of the Christians don't know Jesus. They heard about him, but didn't take time to hear what he said or emulate what he did.

Take a panoramic view of the Christian church and you'll find that racism, segregation, and discrimination is alive and well; all the walls that Jesus fought to tare down, they built them back up and with greater strength than before. The white churches are still white churches and the black churches are still black churches with only a few tokens in either. The bottom line in this is that it is quite understandable from a secular point of view. You see, everybody wants to be around those that they most relate to; so this tendency is quite natural; it parallels with human nature. However, it goes directly against what Jesus taught. In Christ, there is no nationality; we're all one in Christ.

When I study history, I always come across these predators called Christians-the most fierce and dangerous of predators who roam under the guise of religion.

When I studied about the American Indian, I found a group of people who called themselves Christians taking the Indians land. While promising to civilize them and give them some true religion-when the white man says he wants to civilize a people that is his way of saying that he wants to indoctrinate their minds into thinking "white". It is parallel to President Bush saying that he wants to bring the entire world under democracy. I ponder how he is going to do that with other nations when we really don't have true democracy here. Democracy means ruled by the majority. The masses of people don't select a president; the electoral votes do. Do you think for a moment that the masses, with most struggling to live, would allow a mortgage company to charge them three times their purchase, or do you think that the masses would allow banks and financial institutions to charge them 27 percent to 37 percent interest on a credit card; no, they would make it illegal. No, the masses are very unhappy with it. The rich determine the fate of the country, thereby determining the fate of the masses. I wonder, if we cannot function under true democracy, how do we expect other nations that are truly dictatorial, socialistic, communistic, and imperialistic to become something that we have not even mastered.

When I study about the black man and try to learn the intrinsic reason why blacks are treated with such malice, once again its roots are traced back to the hypocritical Christian. They traveled thousands of miles to Ghana, the gold coast, for gold and slaves.

Now picture this, a few ships of white Christians land off the west coast of Africa. Like the Indians, the Igbo tribe welcomed them with open arms. They said that they wanted to give the Igbo civilization and religion-thus history is made. Can't you see the white Christians with chains around the Igbo's neck and feet while telling them, "We're going to give yall some religion and show yall a new world, and incidentally, we're taking all your gold and diamonds with us."

Their Christian religion allowed them to attend worship service on Sunday morning and lynch or burn black families during the night. What hypocrisy; their religion allows them to blow-up abortion clinics and kill many innocent people—killing in the name of religion and justice. Kill the doctor and anybody else that is just a by stander, or someone passing by at the wrong time. Jesus said that we don't commit sin so that "good" will come.

Abraham Lincoln, to appease his countrymen, on both sides of the slave issue, stated that a black man will never equal a white man. He said that the United States could not continue divided. Many thought that he was talking about blacks and white. No, he was speaking of the North and South-the union cannot be divided.

Well, my sentiments are, we cannot continue divided. We must come together-black and white, and make our nation greater than it is.

We must change the paradigm of many of our adults and youth.

And, we must always realize that we are disciples, and Saints, not little "messiahs".

Woe unto the world because of trouble!
Troubles must come, but woe to that man that causes the trouble

Jesus......Matthew 18:7

Pray that you do not enter
Into temptation

Jesus.......Matthew 26:41

GOOD TALK
Breaking the shackles of debt

Debt is the new era slave master—The twenty first century stocks and shackles. The difference between this slavery and past slavery is debt slavery pervades color barrier, ethnic groups, races, creeds, and classes of people. It enslaves all classes and kinds of people. In the past, the shackles were sometimes rusted, beaten, and battered. The shackles of debt are often times golden, shining, and very tempting. Past slavery was forced upon the people; debt slavery, people willingly rush into. Both slave systems affect each succeeding generation.

Debt has whole nations enslaved. You see, it is a deliberate plot that started long before most of us were born. No doubt somebody sat and thought, sat and thought, and thought, and thought how could they capitalize upon the every day common people-for that is truly where the wealth is (collectively). No individual will ever equal the amount of money the collective masses have, but he can become substantially rich by filtering money from the masses; realizing that fact, he came up with a system call credit-which allows one to spend more than he has even before he gets it. Originally, we were developed under a system called bartering-trading goods for goods, or service for goods, or money for goods. They extended bartering to where it included credit, which is in essence debt.

What they said is to let them pay on credit (a little at a time) and let's charge them for allowing them to pay by this system on time (interest). If one is not careful, they will usually pay more interest on the product than what the product originally cost.

The world, as we know it, is divided into two classes of people—laborers and capitalist. Laborers, unlike what most define as simply hard working or task oriented, are people that sell their service to buy goods to maintain life and entertainment. Although laborers have classes among themselves, all are still but laborers-thus laborers are managers, supervisors, and all other upper management position because all of them work for that capitalist at the top that produces the goods to feed the laborers so that they can buy his goods so that he can produce more goods so that they can buy more etc. It is an endless cycle. Laborers usually never get pass being a laborer and their children grow up to become laborers-for we generally immolate those we are closes to.

Capitalist are the people of great wealth. Believe it or not, they are the ones that dictate the direction of our every day lives. They are able to do this because they possess a mass of capital (money); they have businesses, own masses of land, and own corporations and enterprises. They choose our presidents, governors, senators, and mayors. They would like for you to believe that the common people of our nation choose our leaders (democracy). Their money and their influence push the political system and even turn the wheels of justice.

The "working" difference between the laborers and the capitalist: (1) the laborer, as I have previously stated, himself is a commodity-his ability to do work. He sells his commodity to the capitalist to get money to buy his necessities; after the laborer has fulfilled his necessities, he might have a little left over for entertainment. This trend usually goes on and on for the duration of his life-he sells his strength for money to buy food, clothing and shelter for himself and his family. (2) The capitalist, unlike the laborer, buys two types of commodities, physical strength, and material goods, to produce more commodities (goods and physical strength). He uses his money to buy commodity (physical labor) to produce commodity (sellable goods) to sell for money to buy more labor to produce more commodity to sell for more money—the cycle is never ending. Every time he produces more sellable goods that enable him to buy more physical strength to produce more sellable goods, he always takes a portion off the top for his increasing wealth. The wheels of fortune continue to turn until the capitalist has amassed more wealth than he can spend.

The capitalist, which is usually white, does every thing that he can to perpetuate this uneven trend. He gives the laborer credit cards so that he can more readily Acquire the things the capitalist has.

Note very carefully how the capitalist has designed the system: Credit cards: The setup—Most credit cards want you to pay 2%-3% of the balance each month-they refer to this as "the minimum payment". If you did this on a five thousand dollar credit card balance, with an average seventeen percent annual interest rate, it would take you forty years to pay it off, and you will have paid $ 16,304.00 in interest. Wow!!! If you take the same card with twenty percent annual interest rate with minimum payment, it would take you sixty six years and 28,05.00 in interest to pay it off-what a rip off...........and it's all legal.

The capitalist has it "set up" in most all business establishments. They tell the laborer to refinance, but if he is not careful when he refinance, he'll owe more money for a longer period of time. The only thing he would have done is lowered his monthly payment-what a scam! If you pay only what they ask on your monthly mortgage, at the end of thirty years, you will have paid about four times what the house is worth.

Note now, how the capitalist approach the consumer (laborer). They don't stress how much a product cost because they realize that the laborer probably can't afford it, so rather than stress total price, they only emphasize the monthly payment-the "low" monthly payment, which simply means that they are going to get even more money from you.

The system is set-up to keep the laborer shackled by debt; that is the reason why he will loan you money and give you a credit card quicker than he'll finance you a house-a house grows in value. This is why you can see new cars parked in welfare recipients yards, or an expensive car parked in the yard of a run down house-the car usually cost more than the house.

Because the system is such a well organized set-up, it is quite difficult for the laborer to move from laborer to capitalist. One can put all the money in the laborer's hand and it will eventually end up back in the capitalist hands. The reason for this is because wealth starts in the mind first, and then filters to the hand. In order for any laborer to change his condition with lasting effect, he has to first be renewed in his mind-his way of thinking has to change. Just giving people a hand-out doesn't always help. Hand-outs often times stagnates the recipients. This is primary the reason why our prison system fail. Just incarcerating a man doesn't redeem him. Prison time is little or no deterrent, or else our present prisons wouldn't be filled, and we wouldn't be looking for more money to build larger prisons. No, prison is not the answer; it's just "a" means that perpetuates negative results. We must change their mind-set. It has to start before they are of criminal age-most personalities are shaped by the time a child reaches the age of six.

Wealth will always flow in the direction of the generated and regenerated mind. Some folks will acquire a generous portion of money, but won't keep it long because they still have the mind of a laborer—looking for ways to give it back to the capitalist; that's why you have some folks driving a Mercedes Benz while they are struggling to pay the house note and other bills, or they'll pay their credit card bills before they pay their house note. Instead of saving it or investing it, they would much rather give it back to the capitalist, and in so doing, they are allowed to drive cars that they cannot afford.

Athletes fall in the trap sometimes. They'll go from poverty to riches over night. The capitalist are financial wolves looking for financial prey. They attack these young athletes and swindle them out of their money, or they compel them to waist their money on their erroneous, fraudulent capitalistic business venture.

U.S. News magazine did a story on football stars that were ripped off for millions by what they called con men. I found it strange that they only reported on black football athletes-is that to say that whites are never attacked by the financial wolves, or they couldn't find any to report. They reasoned why they chose blacks is because it is expected, the norm, for us to be taken advantage of, or to waist our money frivolously. And, I guest rightly so, from the evidence, we have shown them in the past; they can assume such a mind set.

If we don't change the laborer's mind, he will always be a laborer no matter what he comes to have, for he will always give the money back to the capitalist. If you change the mind, you'll change the end result.

HOW DO I BREAK THE SHACKLES OF DEBT?
Steps to freedom

1. Assess all your debts. You will never get out until you realize how deeply you are in.

2. Stop!! Don't charge anything else. Cut the credit cards up. Stop!! Don't buy any more unnecessary items. You'll find that a great deal of your spending is on what you want rather than what you need.

3. Sacrifice. If you're not willing to sacrifice, you'll not break the shackles of debt. Do you really need a cell phone, a pager, and a house phone? Cut dining out by three fourths. You'll be surprised by how much money you spend on dining out. Stop the shopping; only by what you need. Teach your children to be financially responsible-do they really need that designer whatever? You must cut entertainment. You cannot drink Don Per ion Champaign on a beer budget without suffering a wind fall of debt.

4. Record everything you spend. Put a notebook or tablet in a common area of your home and have everyone write down whatever money is spent on whatever-cokes, candy, dining out, bills, entertainment, etc...........everything!!!! You'll discover some wasteful spending habits.

5. Never ever just pay the minimum payment on credit cards. Always pay more. Even a little makes a substantial difference if you're not continuing to charge. You will notice your balance owed stat to plummet down. As your balance goes down, your minimum payment will also go down. This is the capitalist ploy to keep you in "time" paying the debt-the longer you have to pay, the more you will pay back. So when that minimum payment on your credit cards decrease, continue sending what you previously sent.

6. Pay more on the principle of your house note. Some people think that because they can only do a little then do nothing, but every little bit counts when it comes to mortgage principle. Just twenty five dollars added to your mortgage payment a month will save you thousands of dollars in interest and shorten the time it takes to pay it off.

7. Pay as you go!! Once you pay off your credit cards, charge only what you can pay at billing. In other words, what ever that monthly credit card statement says that you owe, pay it in full.........always a zero balance.

8. When you become free, help somebody else!! One of our greatest faults is that we refuse to help somebody else, or that we are jealous of others.

9. Save and invest!! During your life of work, if you don not pay anyone else, pay God (tithe) and yourself. Each pay period should have going into saving each pay period.

10. Honor God-you cannot accomplish this debt freedom task by yourself; you're going to need supernatural strength to go against society's norm.

THE BORROWER IS ALWAYS SERVANT TO THE LENDER!!!!!

NOTES

NOTES

NOTES

NOTES

978-0-595-37838-8
0-595-37838-2